HOW TO LEARN ASTROLOGY

MARC EDMUND JONES, founder in 1923 of the Sabian Assembly, has had a long-standing critical interest in astrology. He has had professional experience in a wide range of activities, from the Protestant ministry to film editing. His books include *The Guide to Horoscope Interpretation, Astrology: How and Why it Works, Essentials of Astrological Analysis, Occult Philosophy,* and *The Scope of Astrological Prediction.*

HOW TO LEARN
ASTROLOGY

Marc Edmund Jones

SHAMBHALA
Boulder, 1977

Shambhala Publications, Inc.
1123 Spruce Street
Boulder, Colorado 80302

© 1941, 1969 by Marc Edmund Jones
All rights reserved.
ISBN 0-87773-098-9
LCC 76-55119

Distributed in the United States by
Random House and in Canada by
Random House of Canada Ltd.

Printed in the United States

CONTENTS

"Man is not what he is because he was born when he was, but he was born when he was because he was, potentially, what he is."

FOREWORD

ASTROLOGY as here presented is the form of practice on which the majority of astrologers and their students agree, both in America and Europe. Its essence is the use of a horoscope made for the precise place, and for the exact minute and hour as well as the day, month and year of birth. It accepts the methods in calculation and interpretation which have their principal roots in Claudius Ptolemy (2d century A.D.), Didacus Placidus de Titus (fl. 1647–1657), William Lilly (1602–1681), and Lilly's pupil, John Gadbury (d. 1691).

No adequate history of astrology exists, since most of the accounts by its advocates are little more than lists of distinguished devotees in the past, endlessly repeating each other. A real effort to trace out the development and modification of principles and practices in the light of changing social conditions, and in the face of an enlarged human intelligence in all areas of life and science, has yet to be made. The most serviceable historical sketch, at least for the average inquirer, is the unfriendly but competent and informative article on "Astrology" by Charles Singer in the *Encyclopaedia of the Social Sciences,* Volume II, Macmillan, New York, 1931. A valuable account of the astrological literature at the beginning of the twentieth century, listing over fourteen hundred items, is found in F. Leigh Gardner's *A Catalogue Raisonné of Works on the Oc-*

cult Sciences, Volume II, Astrological Books, London, privately printed, 1911.

The writer of this book has long sought an experimental psychology which did not depend on metaphysical assumptions on the one hand, or biological functions on the other, for its basic measurements. Astrology early offered him an attractive possibility, since its frame of reference is wholly astronomical, and he has been at work disentangling its mechanisms from the confusion of its practices since early in 1914.

The book represents definitely pioneer work in astrological instruction. It is the fruitage of three years spent investigating modern teaching methods, through the best facilities offered by the American universities. It starts the beginner with the interpretation of familiar experience at the very outset, and presents the foundations of astrology through a step by step and logical expansion of interest and understanding. Nothing is set out to be learned before it is used. In ordinary pedagogical terms, "learning is by doing."

Thirteen of the twenty-one example horoscopes are from Alan Leo's *A Thousand and One Notable Nativities,* third edition, London, Fowler, 1916. The chart used for Annie Besant is the corrected one to which reference is made on p. 125 of that compilation. Of three charts listed for Martin Luther, Jerome Cardan's is taken.

The horoscopes for Ralph Waldo Emerson, Elbert Hubbard and Woodrow Wilson are from Evangeline Adams' *Astrology, Your Place among the Stars,* New York, Dodd Mead, 1934. Miss Adams' book has many "printings" but no "editions" defined as such, and the charts for Elbert Hubbard and Woodrow Wilson have been corrected from the first "printing" in 1930. The example charts in general are of uneven mathematical competency, but only the more vital errors have been eliminated, since the beginner should be trained from the start to handle the type of material he will encounter in actual practice. Thus, in Elbert Hubbard's chart, the sun and moon are corrected for the exact hour of birth, but the other planets are merely given at their noon positions.

The horoscope for Sigmund Freud is from Mabel Leslie Fleischer, of the Astrologer's Guild, New York; the horoscope of Mahatma Gandhi from George Mc-Cormack, of *Astrotech;* and the horoscope of Pius XI from Margaret Morrell, of *American Astrology.* The horoscopes of the "resourceful lady" and the "Hollywood man" are from the private files of the author.

The information concerning the details in the life of Elbert Hubbard has been obtained from Felix Shay's personal account, *Elbert Hubbard of East Aurora,* New York, Wise, 1926; and Dr. Charles Fleischer, who has known both Elbert Hubbard and Felix Shay intimately, has kindly checked the interpretation according to his own very special understanding.

The pronunciations (but not the respellings, with the consequent use of diacritical marks unfamiliar to the average astrological reader) are from *Webster's New International Dictionary of the English Language,* Second Edition, Springfield, Mass., Merriam, 1935; of which Walter Clyde Curry, Vanderbilt University, is astrological editor. Many of these words are in process of change, however. Usage in the astrological field is often widely at variance with the dictionary preference. Thus the use of "PIE-sees" for "PISS-eeze," and of "You-RAY-nus" for "YOU-rah-nus" is almost universal among American astrologers.

The author is indebted to Lynn T. Morgan for a drawing, and to Dirk Luykx for preparing all the charts and diagrams for reproduction. Invaluable and untiring editorial assistance has been contributed by Margaret Morrell and Mathilde Shapiro.

New York City, September 20, 1940

THE 1969 REPRINTING

When it again became necessary to reprint *How to Learn Astrology* it seemed advisable to revise the mathematics section, partly to provide more recent example charts than the original ones calculated for 1940 and partly because the original text gave considerable attention to what now is a long-discontinued Philadelphia ephemeris in addition to the familiar ones based on the prime meridian at Greenwich. Furthermore, almost three decades of experience in using the manual for the instruction of beginners have come to suggest both an expanded explanation of the details in the mathematical fundamentals of the horoscope and a shift in approach to the use of logarithms.

What might well be noted, at this time, is the extent to which allowance must always be made for changes in the usage or pronunciation of various words. Thus it is interesting to astrologers that the 1961 Merriam-Webster unabridged dictionary now recognizes PIE-sees although listing it as less acceptable than PISS-eeze, whereas the new 1966 Random House unabridged volume prefers PIE-sees and only grants a lesser acceptability to PISS-eeze.

In the later volumes of the Sabian series it has been found advisable to adopt the better-known term satellitium (SAT-el-LISH-ee-um instead of preserving the stellium of John Wilson's 1819 astrological dictionary.

Three paragraphs of discussion of scientific validity and the underlying rationale of astrology, in the original foreword of this book, have been deleted in the reprinting to make room for these added observations. Actually that ground has been covered in much more detail, and in many different connections, in the author's six astrological texts now published after this initial exposition.

Stanwood, Washington, January 28, 1969

HOW TO LOOK AT
A HOROSCOPE

Chapter One

WHAT IS A HOROSCOPE?

A HOROSCOPE is like a picture, or a map. It is not like a page of printing. The way to get at the meaning of a horoscope is to "look" at it, exactly as anyone "looks" through a window, or "looks" over a situation.

Astrologers speak of "reading" a horoscope, but this word often throws the beginner off the track. He thinks he has to learn a series of symbols, like letters to put together in words, and that astrology strings ideas out on a line, like sentences and paragraphs. He tries to store up ideas, ready to link together in this way, and soon gets confused, simply for lack of a correct understanding at the start.

Letters have been invented by men, and words are different in every language, but the elements of astrology actually exist in the heavens. The situation of the stars is transferred, with mathematical correctness, to the sheet of paper. Thus the horoscope is the actual picture of a life as it is represented in heavenly motion.

The astrological "chart," or "figure," or "map," or "wheel," as the horoscope is variously called, is examined in much the same way as the person it represents. Special things may be sought out by the eye, as to see whether the chart has many planets in one place, or whether the person has a large nose (two things that have no astrological connection), but usually any individual is first seen with a whole-view, and a horoscope is handled in the same manner.

The astrological chart uses symbols for the planets. It also identifies certain sections of the heavens as "houses of the horoscope" in one measure of motion, and as "signs of the zodiac" in another. These astrological elements are not many, and they are really easier to learn than many things commonly recognized in seeing a friend, such as the meaning of a smile, a glance or a gesture. The child learns to look at other people by beginning to "look," and to draw conclusions. These conclusions are simple at first. They get more complex only as he grows, and keeps on looking. The astrologer starts in the same way, unless he wants to make everything hard.

The purpose of this book is to help the student to "look" at a chart, accurately and competently, even from the beginning of his study. His first conclusions will be simple, or general, but they will be useful and correct. This will give him confidence, and speed him on his way to a more detailed capacity for judgment.

Here is the regular form of horoscope for a certain resourceful lady. Her husband, a professional man of reputation but great unreliability, left her penniless with four children ranging in age from infancy to seven. She then won a spectacular success, wholly by her own efforts and initiative, and in time became nationally well-known. The beginner, however, will shake his head as he sees this chart.

"How can I look at it and tell anything about it? I don't know what any of the marks mean. All I can see is a sort of large circle, cut up in sections like a big pie, with a small central circle containing information about the place and date of birth."

A similar objection might be made by the baby beginning to "notice" things.

"How can you expect me to tell what's what, when there isn't anything I can recognize, when nothing has any meaning to me?"

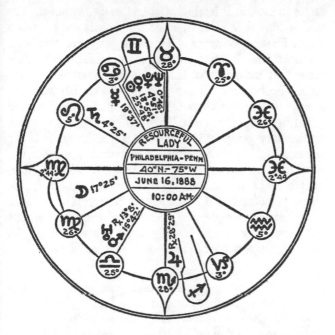

The baby goes right ahead however, and begins to make progress. The astrological infant can do as well, and in the same way.

What is puzzling in this horoscope is the presence of many unfamiliar marks. The symbols for twelve signs of the zodiac are given around the wheel, together with the number of degrees of each which lie on the "house cusps" or spokes of the wheel. Then the symbols for ten planets are found in the houses, with their zodiacal degrees and minutes.

The beginner may well protest, "I'll have to learn the symbols for those twelve signs, right now, and for the ten planets too, and learn what the houses are, and how to use degrees and minutes."

Not at all! The baby doesn't have to learn a lot of facts about this mysterious life around him before he starts to look at it intelligently, and to know things. Life makes him wait, lets him get the details as he needs them. First he is aware of everything as a gigantic blur, more or less. Then he begins to recognize vague patterns that make sense. He builds his knowing step by step. The beginner in astrology should do likewise. As a help to him the chart of the resourceful lady can be given in a different form. This will enable him to get a preliminary grasp of its meaning. Since the symbols for the signs of the zodiac and for the planets and the figures for degrees and minutes are quite unintelligible, simple black marks can be substituted, and the horoscope presented in this elementary but graphic fashion.

At once a simple characteristic of the chart stands out. The black marks actually inside the wheel, "in the houses" as astrologers express it, are as a whole to-

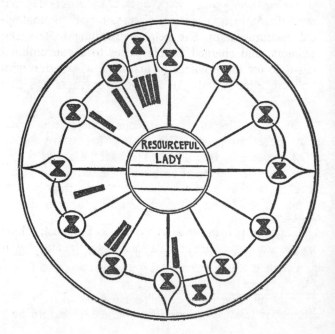

wards the left of the central line. This has a very real meaning in the life of the "native," as astrology calls the person for whom the horoscope is "cast" or "erected." It shows that she can dictate the course of her own career quite completely.

In astrological language, the planets are "east." Thus the beginner must observe that horoscope directions are the exact reverse of those in a map, with east to the left, west to the right, south to the top and north to the bottom.

The native in this case was left absolutely helpless, with her four children, but she didn't waste energy complaining. Instead, she looked around to see what she could do. She was in the artistic quarter of the city, and there she found an unused attic in the hundred-year-old shack occupied by a candy store. In this she opened a tiny shop, selling only cake and coffee but specializing in atmosphere, discussion and psychological encouragement. She helped struggling writers and painters, and charged double prices to a conventional clientele for the privilege of first-hand association with bohemian individuals. In a few short years she had become famous.

This self-direction of the destiny is always shown, one way or another, when the planets are east in a chart. "East" is the section of the heavens where the sun rises, and the area of experience where everything has its start. Now, for a contrast, the beginner can look at the horoscope of Woodrow Wilson, simplified in the same way.

Here the planets as a whole are to the west, which means the exact reverse situation in life. President Wilson was a product of his times, and never the real author of his own destiny. The political developments in the state of New Jersey, with which he had nothing to do directly, were responsible for putting him into

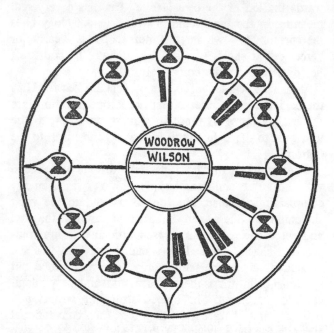

public life in the first place. The nature of the contest in the Democratic National Convention, rather than his own efforts, really led to his initial nomination for the presidency. His first election was due to the split in the Republican party, and his second was only made a fact at the very last minute by the California vote, a surprising outcome of special conditions in the state with which he was wholly unconcerned in any personal way. His international prominence came from the world war, equally apart from his own basic initiative; indeed, his direct efforts for the League of Nations were ultimately unsuccessful to a tragic extent. This is a typical illustration of the life-pattern when the planets lie to the west in the horoscope. Here is where the sun sets in the heavens, and the area in experience where everything has its completion.

To simplify the distinctions made so far, it can be said, somewhat superficially of course, that the emphasis in the eastern half of the chart gives an *à la carte* life, and in the western hemisphere a *table d'hôte* existence. The first type of individual selects his own meal throughout; the other takes what is served him, with only minor choices by comparison.

North and South Distinction

If it is possible to make a distinction between east and west "hemisphere emphasis," as the overbalance of half the wheel is known in astrology, it should be equally possible to distinguish between south and north, or to divide experience on the basis of a sun high in the heavens, or far below the earth. An example of south hemisphere-emphasis is found in the horoscope of Queen Victoria.

When the planets as a whole are south, or above the central line of the horoscope, the life is said to be entirely objective, or concerned only with practical and visible things. This was not only true of Queen Victoria, but of the whole age in which she was a central figure; so that her name has contributed the word "Victorian," or more specially, "mid-Victorian," to the language. The popular idea of this era was that everything must have an outward respectability at the least, and that the under or inner side of life must never be mentioned unnecessarily, or even admitted.

An example, by contrast, of north hemisphere-emphasis is found in the horoscope of Martin Luther.

When the planets as a whole are north, or below the central line of the chart, the life is entirely subjective, or primarily concerned with spiritual and invisible matters. This was dramatically true of Luther. His major

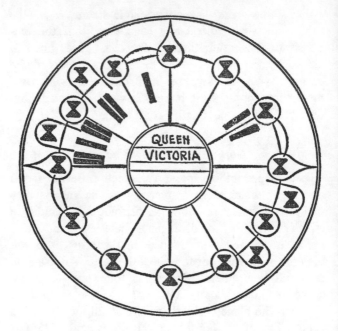

achievement was a reaction against superficial religion, mere outer show of piety, surface conformity to ritual. He definitely stimulated an inner or more true devotion, a faith which would actually be felt and lived. This is demanded by the basic pattern of his chart.

These four cases of hemisphere emphasis are extreme examples, to illustrate the general distinctions. In the charts of Queen Victoria ˙and Martin Luther the planets are actually all on the proper side of the central line. In the case of the resourceful lady, the one planet at the bottom is really on the west side, although by only half a degree, and in the horoscope of Woodrow Wilson the one planet at the top is eight degrees over on the east side. Neither of these variations changes the general situation. In other words, distinctions of this

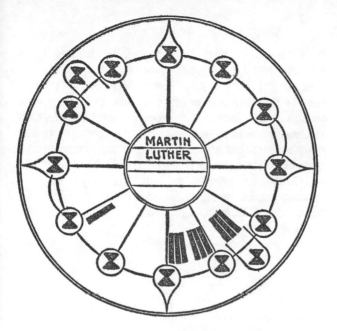

sort are broad generalities. They make it possible to look at a horoscope with an all-at-once or whole view, and so get a first or over-all impression of the person.

The beginner will learn that the characteristics will hold to a lesser extent when the planets have merely a tendency to be all east, west, south or north. It is the same proposition as in life itself. When "tall" or "short" people are picked out, or "fat" and "thin" ones, it then becomes possible to describe others as "somewhat tall," or "slightly fat," and so on. The young astrologer, as he goes on, will have other equally broad means for sorting out people, or describing them in these first complete "looks." He will see that this is the most natural of all ways to approach the interpretation of the horoscope.

Summary

In summary, what has the beginner learned in this first chapter? He has been shown that the way to begin looking at a horoscope is just to look at it, that is, to observe whatever makes sense to him, and to pay no attention to details which he does not as yet understand. He has found that the planets have a tendency to form patterns, and that at least some of these patterns can be recognized or interpreted even before he knows what the planets are, or what the houses and signs mean. As an example, he has been shown how to describe people whose charts have their planets lying to the east, west, south or north.

Chapter Two

WHAT ARE THE HOUSES?

BEGINNERS often make astrology difficult by trying to make everything "different," mysterious or a kind of hocus-pocus. The more unfamiliar anything becomes, the harder it is to learn, to understand or to use. This applies to the houses of a horoscope in particular. Therefore it might be well for the beginner to ask himself, what is a house?

Most simply, a house is a place where someone lives, and in the horoscope it is a place where a planet or a group of planets is located. The heavens are first divided into quarters, or four segments, by the two lines which distinguish between "east" and "west" in the one case, and between "south" and "north" in the other. Then these quarters are each divided into three "houses," so that there are twelve in all.

The idea is that, astrologically, man lives in "many mansions." Each of the twelve indicates one of the many divisions in his experience. He is like the wealthy individual who has a city home for social prestige, a room at the club for times when business alone brings him to town, a country estate in the north for summer and another in the south for winter, a lodge in the mountains for hunting or fishing, and so on. Life has different levels, boundaries and facilities for various ways of acting, and the houses are the first of several means by which astrology measures or reveals man's destiny in terms of the special conditions under which he meets its demands. The degree to which an individual has his life focused or emphasized in one or another of its departments of experience is indicated by the place of the particular planets in particular houses.

The easiest approach to the houses is to see them as an expression of "east," "west," "south" and "north" influences in a horoscope. In other words, the beginner can build on what he has learned in the opening chapter. The arrangement at the east can be shown by a diagram.

The central line pointing east has been shown in heavier inking, and the solid arrow indicates that the house extends from the heavy line, or what is known as the "cusp," in a direction opposite to that moved by the hands of a clock. Incidentally, nearly everything in astrology is taken counterclockwise in this fashion.

The line at the beginning of the easternmost house, rather than the center of the house itself, is pointed directly eastward. The reason for this is that the cusp or threshold of the house has a special significance. It is

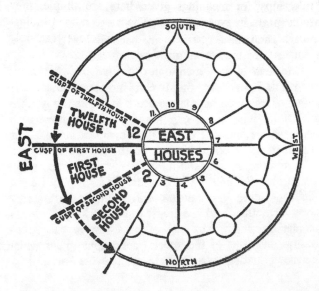

like the front of a building, which represents the whole inside arrangement, and yet does not make the interior any less important.

The primary eastern house is known as the "first house" of the horoscope. Two other houses are more "eastern" than either "northern" or "southern." Thinking always counterclockwise in getting at the basic meaning of astrological details, the house behind the first is known as the "twelfth," and the one in front as the "second." The point of view in this numbering is that of the planets moving through the houses counterclockwise, from the first into the second, and so on. The diagram indicates the span of the twelfth and second houses with a dotted-line arrow in each case.

The Meaning of the Houses

Now what do the houses mean? This is easy to learn if the first chapter has been mastered. While the house "rulerships" or meanings given here are simple, they are accurate in every respect. The more refined indications in the possession of a skilled astrologer are only a further application of these basic relations.

The "east" represents the control of circumstances, or the full and free ability to make decisions. Here is where "a man is a man." Thus the most definitely eastern house, the first, is said to rule or govern "personality."

What the Planets Do

When any planets are "in" a house, they are like tenants who live there. Just as the people dwelling in an actual house will give it color and atmosphere, so planets in the first house give active characteristics to the personality of the native.

There is one planet in this first house, in the chart of
the resourceful lady, and it had everything to do with
the manner in which she built up her business. Because it was the moon, it gave her the approachability
or graciousness which became a large factor in her success. Had it been another planet, she would have solved
her problems no less by her own free efforts, but with a
different "color of personality," according to the nature
of this other planet.

What has been said about planets entirely or largely
east will always hold, and whatever is indicated by a
planet in the first house also will always hold. The many
possibilities of patterns in the chart are matched by an
equally large possibility of combinations in life itself.
Each "look" at a chart is complete, or correct in its own
terms. All the various "looks," if taken carefully and
completely, will be matched by a single confirmation
in the life itself.

Empty Houses

One detail of horoscope interpretation requires
special attention at this point. The beginner will note
that the first house contains no planets in any of the
cases of Woodrow Wilson, Queen Victoria and Martin
Luther. This means that there is no planetary tenant,
but it does not indicate that the person is devoid of
personality. Rather, the presence of a planet in a house
means a special emphasis of the affairs of that house
in the total or "social" life of the individual.

Personality was not in any way an issue in the careers
of these last three. President Wilson was aloof, and the
effort to get him called "Tommy" remained a considerable joke. The queen equally lived in a realm all her
own, whether she shared this with her uncle, later with
her husband, or finally with no one at all for most of

her reign. Martin Luther was a difficult and depressing individual on the personality side. The three had "personality," but the personality was not emphasized as it was in the case of the resourceful lady.

There is a special relationship of some one planet to each of the houses as a ruler or "lord," or as more an owner than a tenant. This will show how the personality is used by the native, whether or not it is emphasized in the primary sense. The point is of no present value to the beginner, however, and its consideration follows more naturally in a later chapter.

The Grouping of the Houses

The central house at the east side of the horoscope, as the place where the native's personality has its astrological indications, is related to a house behind it, and one ahead of it, in a special charting of the personality's activity. Of these the twelfth house rules whatever personality unwittingly carries along with it, and thus it governs the hidden elements in the choices or the self-direction of life. This is for better or worse, as the case may be.

Astrologers call the main or central houses "angular," and the supporting ones behind them "cadent." Thus the first is angular, and the twelfth cadent. What "tags along" with personality can be described as personality's "skeleton in the closet," its lingering moods and fears, or its hidden obligations. This may mean "self undoing," and it may attract hidden enemies, imprisonment and all types of confinement. It also indicates the hidden sources of strength by which the personality builds as well as destroys itself from within.

This twelfth house was most disliked by the old astrologers, with the result that their books paint a rather terrible picture. The fact that it can work as well for good as bad is shown in Queen Victoria's case. The five planets there brought many wonderful things to pass. None the less the major events of her reign were "cadent" in the sense that they took place around and behind her.

The house ahead of the "angle," here the second, is always known as "succedent." This is an unfortunate word, as it emphasizes the secondary or clockwise point of view by which the sun "rises" in the east daily, and by which planets in the second house, carried along by the turning of the whole heavens, will "rise" after those in the first, even though by their own normal motion in the skies they must move on counterclockwise into the third. The succedent house fundamentally is the "prospect ahead," or what lies in store for the native in each of the four basic directions of his life.

The second house rules everything available for strictly personal use. Compared with the twelfth house, where personality is supported, or is both strengthened and weakened out of past experience and general background, the second is where personality expands itself, or where the native "spreads himself" among his fellows. Basically it rules resources, and this among other things is money, or the general medium of exchange by which an individual most easily broadens his experience.

The spreading of personality, or this definite use of resources, is illustrated by the four example charts. The resourceful lady and Martin Luther have planets in the second house. Their careers required that they have the means for free contact with many people and situations. Queen Victoria and Woodrow Wilson, who by contrast were more like the actors in a drama, have no planets in the second. In the latter two instances there was never any real problem of personal means, but in the first two cases the entire lives consisted of a quest for new foundations and resources, financial in the lady's case and institutional in Luther's.

The Houses at the West

The west group of houses includes the seventh as the angle, the sixth as its cadent or supporting neighbor, and the eighth as its succedent or expanding associate. Emphasis of the west side of the horoscope has been seen to be the *"table d'hôte situation"* in general experience. The seventh house, therefore, represents a focus of relationships in which it is necessary to defer to others, or work with others. This most simply is partnership in one form or another. The seventh house, in consequence, rules marriage, and all other coresponsible working arrangements in life, even to sharp competition and open conflict, or opportunity in general.

Queen Victoria is the only one of the example cases with a planet here, and she is the only one of the four

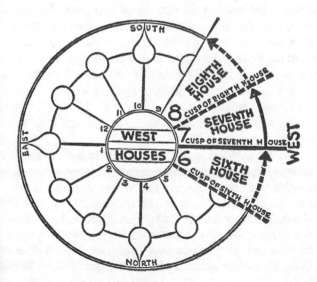

who had to work in strict cooperation with the wishes and desires of someone other than herself. This was exceptionally exaggerated in her early years.

A curiously dramatic illustration of the way in which the horoscope can be interpreted by intelligent "looking," taking each judgment simply and completely by itself, is found in the fact that Woodrow Wilson's chart was initially understood by noting how all his planets are west, and is further delineated now by noting how his seventh house, the most "west" of all the twelve, has no planets in it. Thus his life is quite "westlike" in every respect, but with its "westness" never the basis for a struggle. In other words, the American president was a remarkable example of an individual swept along by a species of broad destiny, and yet he was never sensitive to anything of the sort; it was never an issue in his mind.

The sixth house, as the "support" of these general partnerships with others, rules the type of relationship which has become hidden or limited, for better or worse, on the analogy of the twelfth house. The sixth, therefore, becomes the house of servant-relations, indicating both the people who wait on the native and the attentions he must give to others as a "servant" in turn. It also indicates the direct service he must give to his own affairs, as this takes the form of "work" or becomes a personal maladjustment in the form of "sickness."

Woodrow Wilson, of the example charts, alone has planets here, and his whole career was one crisis after another over his "servant relation" to those about him. The dramatic climax was the historic battle over the Versailles treaty and the League of Nations. He was not, like Queen Victoria, a partner with a governing ministry. Neither the resourceful lady nor Martin Luther found any issue whatsoever in the question of whom they should serve, and how; or who in turn should wait on them, and carry out their wishes.

The eighth house, as the expanding possibilities of partner relations, rules legacies, or the means made available by others for the spread of personality. It thus has considerable analogy to the second house. As the partner-aided spread of personality it governs regeneration, or the development of character along the lines of ideals held by other people; and also rules death as a final chapter in regeneration. The old astrologers found this house almost as difficult as the twelfth, and in consequence said that it was an unfortunate place for the planets. Actually the meaning of the house is quite simple. It always indicates how the native can help others, or how they can help him, in any genuinely reciprocal relationship.

Queen Victoria and Woodrow Wilson have planets here, and this reciprocal activity was a matter of great concern in their lives. In fact, both were chief executives of countries at a time of great change, or unusual national development. Both had much to do, whether directly or indirectly, with a sudden expansion in the destinies of their respective peoples. On the other hand, nothing of this sort was at issue in the careers of the resourceful lady, or of Martin Luther. They were both essentially individualists, quite unmoved by any personal sense of obligation to other people or groups.

The Houses at the South

The south group of houses includes the tenth as the angle, the ninth as its cadent or supporting neighbor, and the eleventh as its succedent or expanding associate. Emphasis of the south hemisphere, or what astrologers often term "all planets above the earth," has been seen to indicate a wholly objective life; that is, one lived in the outer or visible give-and-take of everyday experience. The tenth house rules the general position of the native among his fellows, or his struggle to gain and maintain such a position, and so most simply governs "place in life." This is sometimes described as "honor."

It will be observed in the example charts that there is no emphasis here for Martin Luther. His position in life was assured by the fact of his priesthood, and so it was never an issue. The planet in the cases of Woodrow Wilson and Queen Victoria indicates that the president had to struggle in order to hold the place into which he was catapulted by events, and that the queen faced real problems in giving the British monarchy the new foundation in influence for which she was largely responsible. The great number of tenth-house planets in the chart of the resourceful lady is indication of the special degree to which this one out of the four example cases felt impelled to carve out a real position of her own.

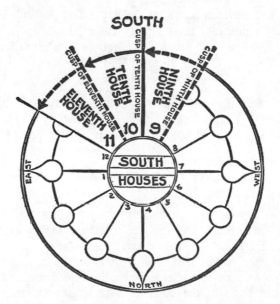

The ninth house, as the support of the place in life, most simply rules "knowledge" or "understanding"; the wisdom by which an individual retains his proper place among his fellows. This involves ideas in nearly every form, and astrologers therefore look to this house for indication of religion and conscience. It shows the intellectual or abstract tie with things at a distance, as well as any practical efforts made to realize or maintain these ties, and it includes the travelling which involves a definite change of base, both temporary and permanent, or what astrologers identify as "long journeys."

Because none of the four example charts have planets in this house, none of these people experienced critical issues of understanding, or of distant associations, in any real sense. This means that each, in his own mind, knew exactly what he was about; that no one of them felt under any necessity to question his own intellectual background.

The eleventh house, as the expanding possibilities of public position, most simply rules friendship in personal terms, and hopes or objectives in a more impersonal way. Queen Victoria and the resourceful lady are the two, out of the example cases, with keen sensitiveness to their need for a real response to their ideals and efforts; and they are the only ones with planets in this house. They alone recognized the existence of a problem in their public acceptability. The queen sought to establish the real influence of the monarchy and the resourceful lady wished to build good will for her business enterprise. Neither Woodrow Wilson nor Martin Luther had any critical concern over their own goals as such, and they were unaware of any problem in the direction of their efforts. Both were obsessed with the creative tasks which engrossed them, and inclined to expect an almost unquestioned acceptance of their accomplishments by everyone around them.

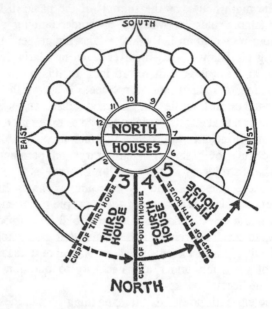

The Houses at the North

The north group of houses includes the fourth as the angle, the third as its cadent or supporting neighbor, and the fifth as its succedent or expanding associate. Emphasis of the north hemisphere, or of "below the earth" affairs, has been found to indicate a specially subjective experience, and this is centered at the fourth house as ruler of the inner or private life of the native, in direct contrast with the tenth house. The rulership is most simply expressed as "home." It is also the "end of life," or the end of any cycle of events, when the values of the experience are established for all to see; i.e., the stage when things "come home" to people, or have their final influence. In this connection the house is often said to indicate the native's soul.

Queen Victoria, alone of the four example cases, has

no planets here. There was not only no real issue, as far as her own inner impulses or subjective doubts were concerned, but the rigid discipline of her upbringing was planned deliberately to eliminate anything of the sort. A pressing sense of deeper necessities, and of very great problems in end-results, was a dynamic driving force in each of the other three individuals, even though this was a very personal or narrow matter in the instance of the resourceful lady.

The fourth house, as ruler of the home, and the tenth, as ruler of the public life and business relations, are together the indicators of the parents. There is considerable dispute among modern astrologers over which house rules which parent, and the beginner will have to make his own ultimate choice. In general, however, it is safe to say that whichever parent touches the native most importantly in terms of his place in life is indicated at the tenth house, and whichever one influences him more through the deeper and inner stirring of the soul is indicated at the fourth.

The third house, as the support of the "home," rules the general familiar and practical surroundings of the native, or indicates his "environment." This includes brothers, sisters and all blood relatives other than parents and children. It embraces all the conveniences of everyday existence in a most complete way, from means of communication to tools of every sort. Books are included on the one hand, and transportation on the other. Thus the house reveals the movement around the normal vicinity in what astrologers call "short journeys."

None of the four example horoscopes have planets in the third house. Like the ninth, this was a department of life in which issues were never raised, in which there was never need for real questioning in any of these cases. Here were people thoroughly settled within their own being, as far as their ordinary surroundings were concerned. The petty details of their efforts were never a problem.

The fifth house, as the expanding possibility of the inner or deeper side of life, rules the native's basic "self-expression." It indicates amusements and relaxation as well as artistic or "creative" efforts. "Home" potentiality may take the form here of speculation and gambling, in an anticipation of values, or it may govern courtship and children as a tangible effort to expand the values which are already embodied in self.

Martin Luther and Woodrow Wilson have planets in this house, which shows that they sought to make a creative contribution to their age, and that their self-expression was a matter of real issue. This would hold no less in failure than in success, as illustrated in Wilson's effort to set up a league of nations. Queen Victoria and the resourceful lady, on the other hand, faced no problem at this point. Neither of them had any genuinely creative sense of a work to do, or of new ground to break, such as was true of the two men; they merely sought to do well what many others had done before them.

Summary

In summary, what has the beginner learned in this second chapter? He has found that the directions east, west, south and north, by which he has been able to make his first steps in looking at a horoscope, are the basis for a division of the heavens into four parts. He has seen that the four quarters are each divided further into three houses of the horoscopes, making twelve in all. He has found that when planets rest in these houses, the corresponding departments of life are shown to be at a stage of issue or crisis.

He is ready now to distinguish the planets, one from another, so that he can give more specific judgments about the native. In the meanwhile he has learned the fundamental meanings of the houses, and it will pay him to review these very carefully before undertaking the next step in astrological understanding.

TABLE OF HOUSE MEANINGS

First	Personality
Second	Resources, Money
Third	Environment, Brethren, Communication, Short trips
Fourth	Home, End of life, Deeper-link parent
Fifth	Self-expression, Speculation, Children
Sixth	Servants, Service, Sickness
Seventh	Partnerships, Competition, Opportunity
Eighth	Legacies, Regeneration, Death
Ninth	Understanding, Religion, Long Journeys
Tenth	Place in life, Profession, Outer-link parent
Eleventh	Friends, Hopes, Objectives
Twelfth	Hidden support and limitation

Chapter Three

WHAT ARE THE PLANETS?

IN the same way that man has his experience in many different "houses," so he has many ways of acting, or different "skills," with which to meet the needs of experience. These are indicated in a horoscope by the planets.

The planets are the bodies that move against the background of fixed stars in the heavens. They form the patterns, by their position in the houses and signs, through which the horoscope has its correspondence to human affairs. Ten are commonly used by astrologers. Mars, Jupiter, Saturn, Uranus, Neptune and Pluto have paths of motion in the sky farther from the sun than the earth's own orbit, and in that order. Venus and Mercury have their paths between the earth and sun. The moon, which circles the earth directly and closely, is an important "planet" astrologically. The sun, which has an apparent motion, due to the fact that all these heavenly movements are observed or measured from the earth, is the tenth and most vital "planet" of all.

The ten bodies are placed in the horoscope exactly as they lie in the heavens, and as they are seen from the earth-center point of view, but they are indicated by symbols which the beginner now must learn. Except in the case of the recently discovered Uranus, Neptune and Pluto, these symbols are combinations of three basic elements. First is the circle, which represents spirit or the limitless "source" of life. Second is the cross, which by contrast stands for simple matter or lifeless substance. Third is the crescent or half circle which is the linking of spirit to life through experience, and is the development of a personal sensitiveness or "feeling" which in astrology becomes a representation of "soul."

The easiest way to learn the meaning of the planets is to look at specially selected horoscopes in which each planet in turn is brought to special prominence. In such a case the life of an actual person will illustrate the planet's significance far better than any description in words. The beginner has mastered the houses in preliminary but thorough fashion through the "hemisphere emphasis" in outstanding example charts. Now he can be helped by a reverse hemisphere emphasis, or by cases where only one out of all the planets is east, west, south or north. This situation is known as "singleton."

The location of a lone planet in a hemisphere gives it an exaggerated influence, on the principle that anything set off by itself has special importance. At times a singleton planet will seem to dominate all the other nine together. The native's whole character will be given a pointed emphasis in the affairs of the singleton's hemisphere. This makes it possible to observe the particular genius of any given planet by taking the case of some well-known person where it is a singleton.

Mars

The symbol of Mars is the cross of matter placed over the circle of spirit, and in practice the cross is made like an arrow-head. This indicates a way of acting in which practical things are more important than ideal ones. It describes activity in its most tangible form. The position of Mars in the horoscope reveals the pat-

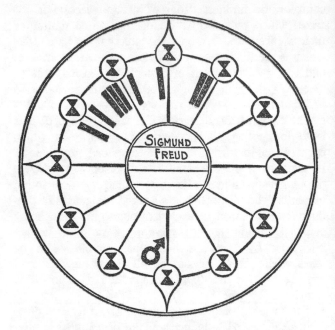

tern of initiative, or shows how the native ordinarily will start anything.

The example chart is Sigmund Freud. His northern hemisphere is given basic importance by a singleton Mars. The fact that Mars is his most important planet makes him a pioneer, and the fact that his northern hemisphere is emphasized means that, like Martin Luther, his work is concerned with the inner side of life. As a matter of record, no other man in human history has done as spectacular a job of pioneering in the hidden depths of personality. Thus he gives an excellent dramatization of this planet's fundamental nature.

Moreover, the beginner may note in passing that Mars lies in the third house. This house rules ordinary environment, and shows that Freud's pioneer work has to take place in the affairs of everyday living. What he started was a technique for adjusting every individual to the normal situations around him.

Jupiter

The symbol of Jupiter is the cross of matter supporting the crescent of soul on its left or east arm. This indicates a way of acting in which the individual selects the circumstances of his self-expression, or. in which the soul acts "eastwardly" by its spontaneous and often "jovial" participation in life. The position of Jupiter in the horoscope reveals the pattern of enthusiasm, or shows how the native ordinarily will invite experience or expand his relationships.

The example chart is Bismarck, one of the astute

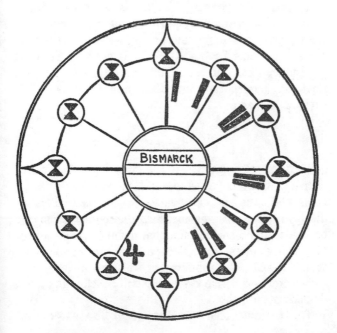

statesmen of the nineteenth century. The fact that Jupiter is a singleton makes this native particularly sensitive to responsibility. The fact that his eastern hemisphere is emphasized means that, like the resourceful lady, he is the executor of his own opportunity. Moreover, the place of Jupiter in the third house means that, like Freud, he works with potentialities immediately at hand. His life dramatically reveals Jupiter's fundamental power of organization, or capacity for enlisting the fullest cooperation of others.

Singleton Near the Hemisphere Line

The beginner will note that the singleton is not directly vertical to the hemisphere containing the other planets, and that this makes no difference in its operation. He should wonder, however, how this case differs from that of Woodrow Wilson, where a planet was eight degrees across the line. In contrast with the former case, Bismarck's Jupiter is in a different sign from the hemisphere line, almost a full thirty degrees into the singleton hemisphere; the distinction is effective because it is sharp.

Saturn

The symbol of Saturn is the cross of matter placed over the crescent of soul, and in practice both the cross and crescent are somewhat modified. This indicates a way of acting in which the individual accepts experience, or in which the soul definitely adjusts itself to practical facts. The position of Saturn in the horoscope reveals the pattern of this sensitiveness, or shows how the native ordinarily will develop any depth of understanding.

The example chart is Havelock Ellis, whose work

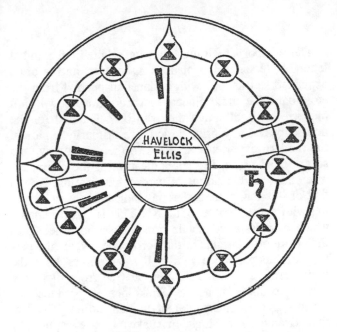

was important in bringing human biological differences into a true psychological perspective. The fact that Saturn is a singleton makes him particularly sensitive to the deeper significance of experience, as well as more than usually aware of common or superficial inhibitions. The fact that his western hemisphere is emphasized means that, like Woodrow Wilson, he is not only a product of circumstances largely beyond his control, but is also denied any real sense of achievement during his own lifetime. Moreover, the place of Saturn in his sixth house indicates his life-work with the maladjustments and sickness of mankind. His life, in terms of its sensitiveness, its depth and its withdrawal from transient and unimportant activities, gives a remarkable insight into Saturn's nature.

Uranus

The symbol of Uranus had its origin in the initial letter of Herschel, the planet's discoverer, and is often explained as this "H" with a planet suspended from the cross-bar. The three planets that were not known until modern times, although they can be calculated for the horoscopes of any prior period, are primarily a part of the modern experience that led to their discovery, and so are most useful in their indication of the characteristic affairs and relations of modern civilization. As the first of the new planets, Uranus indicates a way of acting with special social initiative. This is the originality which a widespread civilization makes possible. Thus the position of Uranus in the horoscope reveals the pattern of independence in the life, or shows how the native ordinarily will keep himself free from dictation.

The example chart is Shakespeare, perhaps the world's greatest interpreter of human nature. The fact that Uranus is a singleton makes him exceptionally detached from the people and conditions around him, and the fact that the planet was not discovered until nearly two centuries after his death is reflected by the different conception of his work in his own age and in present times. The fact that his northern hemisphere is emphasized means that, like Luther and Freud, he reveals a special understanding of the hidden side of life to the modern or Uranus-conscious world, although in his own day he lived wholly objectively under a southern "hemisphere emphasis," and so produced his own plays very "commercially." The place of Uranus in the fourth house means that his most vital concern is with the true roots or "home nature" of men generally, however unsuspectingly this may have been on his own part.

The beginner may note that the uncertainty concern-

ing the details of Shakespeare's birth and life is of dramatic interest here. In other words, the extent to which this horoscope "fits" Shakespeare's life is an important illustration of the fact that any tradition about a man, in order to survive at all, must have as reasonable an astrological basis as any actual history. Here is an almost spectacular revelation of the planet's power to cut across all the lines of lesser or trivial realities.

Neptune

The symbol of Neptune is the trident or three-pronged fishing spear which was long the special emblem of the god from whom the name was taken. Neptune's discovery followed the discovery of Uranus, and its meaning must follow the significance of Uranus, and be derived from the modern experience to which both correspond. After originality, always, come the consequences of the original action, and this is social responsibility. Neptune indicates a way of acting by which the individual fits himself into the civilized mode of life in which he realizes his freedom. This is bondage, when it is not understood, otherwise it is willing conformity to the needs of the group. The position of Neptune in the horoscope reveals the pattern of social obligation, or shows how the native ordinarily will conform to the general desire of his fellows.

The example chart is Pius XI, the most important of modern rulers in the Roman church, and an excellent case because his birth followed the discovery of the planet within a decade. The fact that Neptune is a

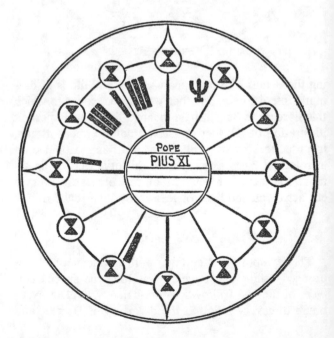

singleton endows him with a high sense of social responsibility, and makes it possible for him to carry out the great new orientation in Catholicism as this was specially symbolized by the establishment of Vatican State. The fact that his western hemisphere is emphasized means that, like Woodrow Wilson and Havelock Ellis, he works with events largely beyond his control. Thus, despite his achievements, he was weighted down to the end by his inability to contribute effectively to world peace. The place of Neptune in his ninth house means that his most vital concern is with understanding and religious values. His marked fidelity to these is a striking illustration of Neptune's dynamic sense of obligation.

Pluto

The symbols for Pluto are many, ranging from a modified "Pl" and the character for Mars with an extra stroke to the circle of spirit placed in a chalice of experience. This latter symbol is an adaptation of an old alchemical idea, to suggest that the planet has a refining function in human affairs. The four commonly used of these symbols are shown in the example chart. As the third and most recently discovered planet, Pluto indicates a way of acting in response to the latest social "trends," or describes the individual's cooperation with the widening possibilities in civilized society. The position of Pluto in the horoscope reveals the pattern of impressionability, sensitiveness to group moods, or shows how the native ordinarily will rationalize his own relations to society at large.

The example chart is Sir William Rowan Hamilton, a mathematician and astronomer of wide and original brilliance. The fact that Pluto is a singleton makes it possible for him to deal with the pure ideas or theoret-

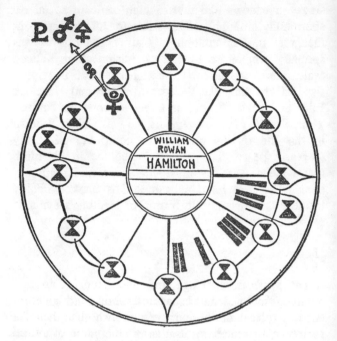

ical relations with which modern science is most concerned. The fact that both his south and east hemispheres are emphasized means that he is enabled not only to establish his achievement solidly in an objective world, but also to be the entire director of his own accomplishment. Moreover, the place of Pluto in his eleventh house means that his vital concern is with objectives, giving him an exceptional direction of his effort to definite ends.

The fact that Pluto was not located until 1930 limits the examples of achievement among those born since its discovery, but in Sir William's chart the singleton Pluto is a genuine indication of the scientific anticipations which characterized his life, and of his power for reasoning in a complete detachment from every immediate situation of his own time, because all this takes on its real meaning and perspective after Pluto's discovery. Here is an excellent revelation of the planet's actual nature, as it is more normally evident in present-day scientific investigation.

Venus

The symbol of Venus is the circle of spirit placed on top of the cross of matter. This indicates a way of acting in which ideal things are more important than practical ones. It describes action in the terms of its contribution to values. This may be relaxation and satisfaction on the one hand, or repudiation and ultimate distaste on the other. The position of Venus in the horoscope reveals the pattern of simple pleasure and appreciation in the life, or shows how the native ordinarily will finish things, and give them meaning.

The example chart is a Hollywood man of prominence, typical of those individuals whose esthetic development particularly dramatizes the nature of Venus. The fact that this planet is a singleton reveals him as extremely impatient with outworn or commonplace ties, and passionately devoted to pleasure or the experience of the beautiful in every phase of intimate human relationship. The fact that his eastern hemisphere is emphasized means that, like the resourceful lady, Bismarck and Sir William Hamilton, he is the actual architect and administrator of his own destiny. Moreover, the place of Venus in his tenth house means that he is able to capitalize handsomely upon his esthetic talents in the motion picture field, affording a neat and sharp illustration of this planet's nature.

Because the two planets inside the earth's path in the solar system, Venus and Mercury, have relatively small orbits, they cannot get very far away from the

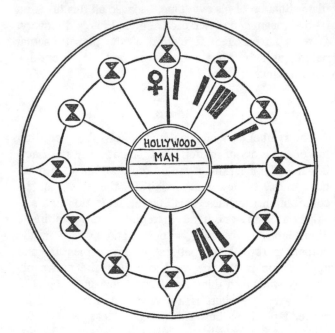

sun, and the sun is always closely associated with them
in consequence. This means that singleton cases for
any of these three bodies are not only rare but unsatis-
factory, since they may usually be taken equally well or
even more naturally as simple hemisphere-emphasis.
The Venus example just employed is an excellent case
of the planet's influence, but it should be obvious even
to an inexperienced astrologer that the picture of an
esthetic control of the life, under this eastern hemisphere singleton, is matched by an equally valid conception of a man held to a *table d'hôte* limitation of experience, in any ordinary everyday sense, by his very
overbalanced interest in esthetic things. This latter view
of his career is held by his family, who have no sympathy at all with any of the ideals expressed in the

Venus singleton. Here again the young astrologer may
see how all the proper "looks" at a horoscope will be
reconciled and confirmed in the single unified fact of
the actual life.

The Moon

The symbol of the moon is the simple crescent of
soul, and this is significant because there is neither
modification of the symbol nor suggestion of limitation
upon the soul. The moon indicates a way of acting in a
wholly unashamed self-interest. It describes the inner
rehearsal of experience by the soul, and also the resulting wholly individual activity through which the native
remains a distinct personality among his fellows. The
position of the moon in a horoscope reveals the pattern
of the soul's inner response, usually called the "feelings" in sharp distinction from the sensitiveness of understanding under Saturn, or shows how the native ordinarily will establish himself in everyday affairs
through his emotional, common and public characteristics.

The example chart is Sir Richard Burton, famous
translator of the *Arabian Nights,* as well as noted ad-
venturer in India and the Near East. The fact that the
moon is a singleton gives him the gift for a complete
emotional placing of himself in any chosen reality.
Thus it was possible for him to disguise himself and
make the pilgrimage to Mecca in days when discovery
as an intruder was sure death. The fact that his southern hemisphere is emphasized means that, like Queen
Victoria and Sir William Hamilton, he is utterly un-
disturbed by inner complications, and is able to direct
the whole of his energies to a given task of the moment. Moreover, the place of the moon in his eleventh
house means that, like Sir William again, his vital concern is with objectives, or the definite direction of his

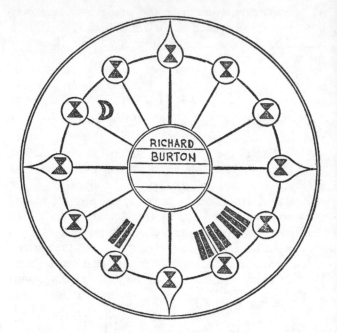

efforts to tangible ends. The degree to which he was so strikingly a "personage" is excellent dramatization of the moon's fundamental character.

In passing, the beginner may note that Pius XI has a north singleton planet as well as his west singleton Neptune. This is the moon, and it shows the spiritual kinship between the pope and Martin Luther in the north, as well as between the pope and Burton in the emotional completeness with which they could give themselves to whatever enterprise engaged them, under the moon singleton. The Neptune emphasis in the case of Pius has been more valuable for illustrative purpose, but the moon singleton is more sharply defined, and would be of greater primary value in any personal delineation of that native's life.

The Two Remaining Planets

The meaning of the sun and Mercury, which remain, is approached more effectively by different techniques, in each case, than the singleton charts. Their symbols, however, can be analyzed in the same fashion as the others.

☉

The Sun

The symbol of the sun is the circle of spirit with a dot or "period" in the middle. This indicates a way of acting in which spirit, as the central "self" or will, is made evident in experience. The position of the sun in the horoscope reveals the pattern of the will, or shows how the native ordinarily will seek to strengthen his own personal integrity.

☿

Mercury

The symbol of Mercury is the crescent of soul placed in the form of a cup on the circle of spirit, which in turn has been placed on the cross of matter. This indicates a way of acting in which the supremacy of idea over material things is made personal. It describes the continuing use made of the things finished or given meaning under Venus, which most simply is the awareness and ordering of various factors in experience, or basic mentality. The position of Mercury in the horoscope reveals the pattern of "mind," in an important distinction from the driving determination of "will," or shows how the native ordinarily will know the circumstances of his situation.

Mercury's Function

The fact that Mercury and the sun must always remain close to each other in the skies is the real basis of Mercury's function in astrology, and this suggests the technique by which the beginner may gain an effective idea of the planet's nature. The sun is the central body of these two, exactly as the "will" is central in man. Mercury, by contrast, is continually changing its relationship. Now it presses ahead of the sun, and now it falls behind. Man's "mind" in the same way is now ahead of his situation or affairs, and now behind. The working of the "mind" is much like the activity of a youngster out walking with his father. There are times when he runs ahead to investigate this or that, only to drop back for support or encouragement, and other times when he lags behind in a moment of concern over some fascinating aspect of things, until it is necessary to hurry forward and catch up again.

The only important difference between one mind and another is the underlying or general tendency of one individual to reach forward and anticipate things, and of another to lean back and recapitulate them, together with the further distinction by which some minds do this in rather an extreme degree, whereas others remain relatively close to the central balance of will. Mercury in this fashion indicates four types of "mentality." The identification of these types, among the twelve example cases with which the beginner has been concerned, will give him an excellent conception of the planet's function in astrological delineation.

The older astrologers distinguished Mercury's position on the basis of its clockwise "rising" ahead of the sun, rather than its counterclockwise "moving" ahead of the sun. In other words, when Mercury is a morning star it is "ahead," and when it is an evening star it is "behind." This form of expression is too well set in practice to be changed.

If Mercury is "ahead" of the sun in this respect, that is, swinging away from it in a clockwise direction, the native's mind is "eager." If it is more than fourteen degrees ahead—that is, more than half its possible distance—the mind is not only eager, but is also untrammeled. Then the mind is like the little boy when he is far enough ahead of his father to feel altogether free to examine everything, and to deal with everything, quite in his own imperious way. Queen Victoria, of the four cases in the first chapter, is the example of this. Her life was not only wholly objective, but she was able to see everything objectively in her mind, and to make her decisions and guide her own movements without interference from any inner reaction or feeling. She was exceptionally alert to her responsibilities as queen, and was interested in their full detail with an almost child-like ingenuousness. In the eight charts of the third chapter, those of Bismarck, Havelock Ellis and Shakespeare all indicate this untrammeled eagerness of mind. They also were able to approach life with a real mental objectivity, easily evident in the work of Bismarck and Shakespeare but no less marked in the scientific clarity and wit of Ellis.

When Mercury rises ahead of the sun in the natal chart by less than fourteen degrees, the mind is eager but is more will-censored or self-conscious. This is illustrated, in the four original examples, by Martin Luther, but by no one at all in the eight following cases. Luther pushed on ahead of his fellows in his spiritual battle, but he no less leaned back almost desperately for support in the tradition of the church. This confirms the north hemisphere emphasis of his chart, as in contrast with the southern placing of the planets in the queen's horoscope. Luther wanted to reform the evil ways of the church, but he had no desire to start a new organization, or to plunge forward into any unknown depths.

When Mercury rises behind the sun, swinging away from it in a counterclockwise direction by more than fourteen degrees, the mind is "deliberate" rather than eager, and in the extreme of this separation is also "untrammeled." The resourceful lady is an example of this "mental chemistry." Her thinking, like that of Queen Victoria's, is without self-sensitiveness. This is a characteristic which is reinforced in her case by the eastern hemisphere-emphasis. At the same time her mind is deliberate, or careful. She took good account of lessons from the past, and gave attention to the general store of human wisdom. Differing from the queen, she anticipated nothing but instead viewed life in a continual recapitulation. To her, the more it changed the more it was the same thing. Her mentality is like that of William Rowan Hamilton, whose case is the one parallel among the eight charts used to introduce the planets. Sir William, despite his work a full century ahead of his time, saw the future of knowledge as only a clarification or refinement of materials already possessed in one aspect or another.

The fourth type of "mental chemistry" is the deliberate mind which is self-conscious, indicated when Mercury rises behind the sun by less than fourteen degrees.

Woodrow Wilson is the example of this, with his ever-evident historical background, or his personal sensitiveness to the lessons of history. Because no problem arose in his focal dealing with others at the seventh house, he uncritically felt himself to be the very agent of history itself. This form of mental make-up is found also in four out of the eight charts in the present chapter. Thus Sigmund Freud is as essentially personal, dealing with the very roots of self, as Havelock Ellis is scientifically objective, possessing an untrammeled and eager mind. Richard Burton, second of the four cases in question, was self-consciously concerned with the cultural roots of man to an extent which led him into real notoriety, and the Hollywood man buried himself in the deep stirrings of human relations to no less exaggerated a degree, equally against his own interests. Pope Pius XI assimilated his whole personality into the actual body of the church, and almost sought to live its whole history in his own exceptionally sensitive ideals and efforts.

By the time the beginner has been given further example horoscopes, he will be equipped with the simple factors he will need to determine this Mercury-sun relation for himself in any chart. The form in which these earlier examples are presented, except the introductory complete wheel, has given no identification to the planets generally, and no indication at all of the distances separating them. The details of technique would be useless and confusing at this point.

The special consideration of the sun is best approached in a separate chapter, but the whole scheme of the planets is complete, and the beginner will do well to make sure he has mastered the materials thus far given before he proceeds to the next step in understanding.

THE PLANETS AND THEIR SIMPLE MEANING

Arranged in an order of practical convenience

Sun	Purpose
Moon	Feeling
Mars	Initiative
Venus	Acquisitiveness
Mercury	Mentality
Jupiter	Enthusiasm
Saturn	Sensitiveness
Uranus	Independence
Neptune	Obligation
Pluto	Obsession

Summary

In summary, what has the beginner learned in this third chapter? He has found out that if any hemisphere in a horoscope, created at the east, west, north or south, contains a single planet only, known as a singleton, this planet will reveal a dominant way of acting in the native's life. By looking at example charts of singleton emphasis for each of the planets in turn, excepting only Mercury and the sun, he has achieved a preliminary but real idea of their meaning. At the same time he has been introduced to the symbols for all ten of these bodies, together with the implications of the symbolism in each particular case.

He has gained an insight into the nature of Mercury by observing the difference, in the twelve example cases, between those whose Mercury rises ahead of the sun and those whose Mercury rises behind. In each of these two classes he has observed the further distinction between those whose Mercury is relatively distant from the sun and those whose Mercury is close.

He has had further experience in looking at actual horoscopes, and in coming to definite and correct conclusions by the use of the few simple facts he has acquired so far in his study. This should give him an increasing confidence in his own capacity. The example charts have afforded him an additional drill in the meaning of hemisphere emphasis, and in the significance of six out of the twelve houses. He has seen, although to a very limited degree, how exceptions to exact rule are in themselves an indication of importance.

Chapter Four

WHAT ARE THE SIGNS?

IF the houses are the "many mansions" in which man as an individual has his experience, the signs are the similar departments in the heavens by which life itself, or the experience of all men together, is given character and distinction. This means that the approach to an understanding of the signs must be a little different from the means used to give the beginner his initial idea of the houses.

The easiest way to define a "sign of the zodiac" is to identify it as the section of the heavens through which the sun moves during some thirty days of an astrological "month." The sun is always at approximately the same place for the same day of every year because a "year" is the total movement of the sun through these twelve signs. The calendar year begins January first, and the astronomical or astrological year in March, but the same span of time is indicated by both. Therefore the sign in which any person's sun will be found can be learned by merely asking him the month and day of his birth. It is obvious that the sun has a very special relation to the signs, and the simplest approach to their meaning is also the most effective way to understand the nature of the sun itself. For this reason, even more than the lack of charts with a singleton sun, the consideration of the planet has been deferred from the prior chapter.

Two vital factors of the horoscope are created by the regularity of the sun's annual motion through the skies, or by the rhythmic succession of spring, summer, autumn and winter brought about with its swing to the north and then to the south once a year. First, the path in which this motion takes place is given a definite character. It becomes the zodiac. Secondly, these seasons establish common factors of experience among men, and lead to a real dramatization of all human experience in the zodiac. Thus youth is the springtime of life, and old age the winter of experience. Summer is a period when play is brought to a high point, especially in the climax of a vacation. Recreation and amusement become the means by which men increase their social intercourse and add to their common experience, as in the great crowds at various contests and the interest in sports generally. Autumn and harvest bring about a different tempo of existence, so that even in city life there is the opening of a new "year" in business, a new term in school, a new season in the theatre, and so on. The Christmas and New Year holidays give a turn to deeper or inner things for most people, and unpleasant weather helps magnify home affairs, personal ties and spiritual values.

The beginner need not attempt any deep study of these details, or try to make any philosophical analysis of the various human institutions around him, but he must recognize the basic orderliness or rhythm which underlies every phase of life, and realize that it is constant or predictable, at least in general outline. The zodiac is the pattern of man in this respect. It has its correspondence to affairs on the earth, first in terms of the seasons, and then progressively through a host of relations, all of which have their common foundation in the seasonal distinctions. Ecclesiastes voices a very sound astrology when it remarks, "To everything there is a season."

The Zodiac and the Constellations

The word "zodiac" means "circle of animals," and the name refers to the means taken by ancient astronomers to identify its various parts. Selecting stars that could be connected by lines to give a rude representation of some appropriate figure, they established twelve of these. The original signs, traced out this way in star patterns, are known as the "constellations" or collectively as the "natural zodiac," and they are seldom used in astrology. The reason is that the astronomical point which is taken as the zodiac's beginning has a very slow clockwise movement in the skies. This is known as the "precession of the equinoxes," and it is sometimes used to define the great "ages" of human history. In the more than two thousand years since the zodiacal signs were established, the star-patterns which still name them are found about a whole sign out of position. This fact, not understood by opponents of astrology, is often cited as evidence of its supposed "unscientific basis."

The "animal" designations of the various signs were not only for the purpose of identifying the twelve sections of the heavens, but were also designed to dramatize the successive stages in human experience. The sun as a symbol of the will makes its annual "pilgrimage" through the zodiac and the order of events, or seasons of effort, are visualized as "ordeals" which in one way or another are typical in the lives of all men. This is the concept which took classical form in the twelve "labors of Hercules."

Since each person has his sun at birth in one out of

these twelve divisions of the zodiac, the signs also sort people into twelve classes. Each class gives a special emphasis of some one part of the experience symbolized by the whole annual pilgrimage of the sun, or the will. The idea is that each man is found at some special point in this "pilgrimage" because it affords him the fullest chance to use his particular talents. The resulting concept of twelve basic types among human beings is represented in the twelve tribes of Israel and the twelve apostles.

How the Zodiac Describes Experience

The annual "pilgrimage" of the will is a symbol not only of the ordinary recurrent seasons of experience for all men together, but of the whole span of any given life. It becomes a symbolical gamut of experience. This has already been suggested in the idea of youth as springtime and of old age as winter. This zodiacal wholeness, however, is not merely a sort of longer "year." It is rather the continuing repetition of both beginning and maturity throughout the everyday activities of life. A man begins a little "year" when he wakes in the morning, and also a special "year" when he enters any new experience or launches any fresh enterprise. His capacity to initiate things is an activity of Mars, but it is also a persisting phase of his experience which, apart from its other relations, is permanently represented by the first sign of the zodiac because that is the point of what might be called springtime capacity in his make-up. Ordinary language recognizes this when it speaks of a man "springing" into action.

Astrology requires a tangible means for expressing this form of relationship, and achieves it through the fact that all living organisms have a tendency to grow, and to distribute their functions, in a consistent head-to-foot pattern. The spring-to-winter order of relations in the zodiac has a necessary correlation to this head-to-foot order in natural organisms, and the astrological correspondences are revealed by establishing a hypothetical human body around the heavens in the zodiac. This establishes a direct relationship between a given section of the skies and a particular part of the body, and it is by no means as arbitrary or artificial as it might appear at first glance. The pictorial diagram of this "zodiacal man" is commonly used on kitchen almanacs and in other popular astrological material; a scheme more widely familiar than the horoscope itself.

If the particular sign of the zodiac containing the sun of a particular native is a means for sorting him out into one of the twelve basic "types" of human nature, then it must also follow that he will be sorted out in similar fashion among the possibilities of physical make-up, depending on that part of the universal or heavenly "body" to which his sun-sign corresponds; i.e., his build or functional development will reflect that "season" of general human possibility which he is making particularly his own. This is his "appearance," or the total sum of his physical characteristics; and it is a further and very important matter indicated by the signs. While it is impossible, of course, for one man to look like a head, or another like a knee, yet the sign ruling the head indicates a marked tendency towards a large nose, among other things, and the one corresponding to the knees will usually identify a person with a definitely knotted and angular appearance.

The Importance of the Sun-Sign

In consequence of all this, the most important indication of the signs in the horoscope is through the one which holds the sun. There are nine other planets which have their testimonies to give, according to their own basic activities in the life, and there is also the vital information given by the signs on the cusps of the houses, particularly by those on the four angles. However, the signs are best learned through actual cases in which the sun will emphasize each in turn, first by revealing the fundamental "point" to the life which this particular planet shows, and then by delineating the outer appearance which the sun sign shapes in a basic structural fashion.

The analysis of a native's physical make-up is the greatest single difficulty in astrological practice. The same man will present a different appearance to different people, and will also appear differently according to the occasion and the mood of any moment. He will look taller among shorter companions and will seem more aggressive among less dynamic associates. Distinctions ultimately depend on their familiarity, as is illustrated in the great trouble any individual will have in telling Orientals or colored people apart, unless he has had appreciable experience among them. Astrological "appearance" is a composite of many things, and the position of the sun by sign will indicate only a few among them. These will be of foundation importance, but they will not be easily distinguished from the other factors in actual practice.

In general, the ascendant or cusp of the first house will seem to have a much greater influence on the personal appearance. This will be the superficial everyday modification, but no less a difficulty. The moon's sign is often most important, especially in giving a clue to the native's play of moods and unconscious "play-acting." The beginner must remember that the sun-sign gives a basic tendency only. He must never expect too literal a conformity to what after all can only be general suggestions for the sign, especially when they must be written to apply to all people of a given race and culture.

Summary

In summary, what has the beginner learned in this fourth chapter, as an introduction to the thumbnail sketches of the signs to follow? He has been shown that the signs of the zodiac are created by the regular movement of the sun through the heavens; also that the seasons established by the sun are the basis for the zodiac's distinctions on the one hand, and for the identification of the common or universal elements in human life on the other. He has found that the signs of the zodiac are symbolized by "animal" figures, designed to represent various phases in mankind's experience, and that each one of them also corresponds to some special part of this experience, or creates one of the twelve basic types among human beings.

He has discovered further that the zodiac has a relationship to each individual's whole life, and that the twelve signs will correlate to the persisting types of experience in the given individual's case; so that it is possible to delineate the human body in the skies and make the zodiac a "heavenly man" or "zodiacal man" to represent this relationship. He has seen that the difference in individual appearance is the result of an emphasis upon certain areas in individual experience, and that this is indicated by the sun-sign most fundamentally, but also importantly by the ascendant and the sign containing the moon.

ARIES

The sun is in Aries from March 21st through April 19th. This is the fullness of spring, or the time of year for original and dynamic activity, and it makes Aries the sign of the pioneer. The symbol is the ram, represented by his horns, and expressing the persistence of life's springtime return to activity. Aries in any chart will show a native's capacity to initiate things. In the "heavenly man" the sign indicates the head. It therefore reveals the source of determination and the general direction of a native's efforts.

The sun here describes a fearless individual who is usually able to make his own place in life; who will generally meet any problem with quick and positive action. The beginner has had an example of this in the chart of Bismarck, who made good use of the aggressive genius of the sign, and who demonstrated to his own generation what a real leader could accomplish. A further example of the Aries driving force, in what outwardly was quite a gentlemanly fashion, will be seen in the horoscope of J. P. Morgan. Aries as a factor in appearance tends towards a closely-knit body, medium to tall in height, with a long neck, broad forehead and a narrow chin.

Parenthetically, since the sun's movement from sign to sign will vary slightly from year to year, the dates can only be given approximately.

TAURUS

♉

The sun is in Taurus from April 20th through May 20th. This is the falling away of the springtime drive, or the time for evaluation of the personal energies, and it makes Taurus the sign of stamina. The symbol is the bull, represented by his face and horns, and expressing life's persistent exercise of its powers. Taurus in any chart will show a native's capacity to maintain his everyday interests. In the "heavenly man" the sign indicates the throat and neck. It therefore reveals a native's basic approach to reality in the terms of the materials he takes into his body, and the voice he gives to his reactions.

The sun here describes an individual who is eager for experience, if he can have it on his own basis; who is inclined to be patient and to hold steadfast to his own ideals. The beginner has had examples of this practical temperament, with its accompanying mastery over materials, and its drive for expression, in the charts of Freud and Shakespeare. Taurus as a factor in appearance tends towards a rather filled-out body, ranging from short to medium, with a full neck and emphasized shoulders, a face apt to be round, and a full mouth with dimpled cheeks or chin.

GEMINI

Ⅱ

The sun is in Gemini from May 21st through June 20th. This is the rising anticipation of summer, or the time for marshalling talent and enthusiasm, and it makes Gemini the sign of life-giving. The symbol is the twins, represented by two linked upright lines, and expressing the irrepressible restlessness by which man divides himself and widens his experience. Gemini in any chart will show a native's versatility. In the "heavenly man" the sign indicates the shoulders, arms, and hands, together with the lungs. It therefore reveals the effort of a native either to manipulate experience directly, or to intensify experience by a deeper "breath" of participation.

The sun here describes an individual who is unusually aware of everything around him, and anxious to put it all to use; who is active and cooperative as long as events proceed on a familiar pattern. The beginner has had examples of this common-sense enthusiasm and adaptability in the charts of the resourceful lady, Queen Victoria and Pope Pius XI, and will have further illustrations in the horoscopes of Elbert Hubbard and Ralph Waldo Emerson. Gemini as a factor in appearance tends towards a slender body, inclined to be rather tall, with long lines in features and figure, and to have quite round eyes, a lengthy nose and a wide mouth.

CANCER

♋

The sun is in Cancer from June 21st through July 22nd. This is the fullness of summer, or the time for self-consummation and an abandonment of all restraint, and it makes Cancer the sign of growth. The symbol is the crab, represented by the conventionalized claws, and expressing the self-gathering tenacity by which all life constructs its own actual world. Cancer in any chart will show a native's capacity for rebuilding things. In the "heavenly man" the sign indicates the stomach, the chest and the breasts. It therefore reveals a native's taking and giving of nourishment, or his participation in the general enlargement of all experience.

The sun here describes an individual who has an unusual insight into the possibilities of a situation, and will stick to any course of action to the end; but who can see things only in terms of self-interest. None of the example charts in this book have the sun in Cancer, but Henry VIII and Cecil Rhodes are excellent cases of aggressive self-interest for the beginner to consider. Cancer as a factor in appearance tends towards a broad or stout body, ranging rather short, with marked angles in form or features, and often with a high chest or forehead, also sometimes with an exceptionally round face.

LEO

♌

The sun is in Leo from July 23rd through August 22nd. This is the falling away of the summer fullness of living, or the time for enhancing the values in personality, and it makes Leo the sign of self-sufficiency. The symbol is the lion, represented by his head and mane, and expressing the pride by which all life identifies and preserves its ideals. Leo in any chart will show a native's capacity for genuine self-exaltation. In the "heavenly man" the sign indicates the heart, the upper back and the spine. It therefore reveals the fundamental rhythm of a native's existence, together with the core or center of his everyday morale.

The sun here describes an individual who has a particular gift for dramatizing things, or giving importance to what he does; who can handle any situation he is permitted to dominate. The beginner has had one example in Sir William Rowan Hamilton, the only case of a Leo sun in the book, but further illustrations may be found in Percy Bysshe Shelley, who did not really succeed in controlling his circumstances, and in George Bernard Shaw, who by contrast has dominated his own situation completely. Leo as a factor in appearance tends towards a slender but round body, relatively short in stature, with sleek hips and a head that is usually full, round and even dome-shaped, and occasionally with large or protuberant eyes.

VIRGO

♍

The sun is in Virgo from August 23rd through September 22nd. This is the rising anticipation of autumn, or the time for marshalling social advantages and capitalizing on human contacts, and it makes Virgo the sign of readjustment. The symbol is the virgin, represented by the "M" of primitive matter with an added stroke to suggest a chastity girdle, and expressing the self-concern by which all life sharpens its critical powers. Virgo in any chart will show a native's capacity for cataloguing life and relations generally. In the "heavenly man" the sign indicates the intestines and the abdomen. It therefore reveals a native's power for assimilating the substance of experience, or sorting it out for use.

The sun here describes an individual who enjoys close and routine relationships with other people or things; who particularly likes to put various affairs in place. The beginner will have an excellent example of this tendency to reduce the world to order in the case of Goethe, often called the last universal genius, and an additional case is found in Queen Elizabeth, whose chart does not appear in the book. Virgo as a factor in appearance tends towards a lean but strong body, of great range in stature, with a generally flat and beautiful back and with a wide forehead, square brows and often a very long upper lip.

LIBRA

♎

The sun is in Libra from September 23rd through October 22nd. This is the fullness of autumn, or the time for sharing the fruits of growth and for developing human cooperation, and it makes Libra the sign of equilibrium. The symbol is the scales, represented by the balance, and expressing the power of choice by which all life gains its ends. Libra in any chart will show a native's capacity for stimulating and sharing experience, or for establishing harmony in all relations. In the "heavenly man" the sign indicates the kidneys and lower back. It therefore reveals the subtle extraction of ultimate values from experience, as in contrast with Virgo's more tangible assimilative processes, and this is a native's gift for translating events into knowledge.

The sun here describes an individual who rejoices in adventure and change or revels in the chance to investigate life; who is quick to participate in any event most wholeheartedly, but who is subject to moods and is an extremist in all things. The beginner has had an excellent example of this quick response to the immediate state of things in the Hollywood man, and will have two more cases of its dynamic extremism in Annie Besant and Mahatma Gandhi. Libra as a factor in appearance tends towards a slender body, medium in height, with an oval face and symmetrically lovely features, the figure often sway-back.

SCORPIO

♏

The sun is in Scorpio from October 23rd through November 21st. This is the falling away of the autumnal refinement of experience, or the time for an examination of the values in life, and it makes Scorpio the sign of creative power. The symbol is the scorpion, represented by the "M" of primitive matter with a stinging tail added, and expressing the ability of all life to protect itself from undesired compulsion. Scorpio in any chart will show a native's capacity for developing and strengthening his own creative resource. In the "heavenly man" the sign indicates the eliminative and reproductive organs. It therefore reveals a native's discrimination between the higher and lower aspects of life, and the resulting sense of basic self-respect.

The sun here describes an individual who has real political gifts, and an ability to see deeply into the purposes of others; who is able to turn almost everything to his own account. The beginner has had one example of this high form of social craftsmanship in Martin Luther and another illustration outside the book can be found in the case of Theodore Roosevelt. Scorpio as a factor in appearance tends towards a thick-set, sturdy body, of better than medium stature, with a face inclined to be square and broad, with thick lips and eyes characteristically drooped at the outer corners.

SAGITTARIUS

The sun is in Sagittarius from November 22nd through December 21st. This is the rising anticipation of winter, or the time for marshalling the inner resources of personality, and it makes Sagittarius the sign of distribution. The symbol is the centaur archer, represented by the arrow, and expressing the continual association in life between animal and rational experiences. Sagittarius in any chart will show a native's capacity for unrestricted human relations. In the "heavenly man" the sign indicates the flesh of the entire organism, together with the hips and thighs. It therefore reveals a native's flush of personality, or his ability to give real "body" to his experience.

The sun here describes an individual who has a great love for human companionship, often without any great degree of discrimination; who is yet able to awaken the real aspirations of all other people. The beginner will have no examples of its spontaneous temperament in the book, but excellent illustrations are found in Benjamin Disraeli and Thomas Carlyle. Sagittarius as a factor in appearance tends towards a large body, often marked by fleshiness below the waist, frequently tall, and usually with a handsome face, high forehead, round clear eyes, and a distinct tendency to baldness, at least over the temples.

CAPRICORN

♑

The sun is in Capricorn from December 22nd through January 19th. This is the fullness of winter, or the time for deeper satisfactions and genuine self-restraint, and it makes Capricorn the sign of the critic. The symbol is the goat, represented by the line of his head and horn, and expressing the extreme of creative resource in all life. Capricorn in any chart will show a native's capacity for discrimination. In the "heavenly man" the sign indicates the skin generally, and also the knees. It therefore reveals a native's power to draw experience into the limits of selfhood, and to compel a basic respect for everyday practical values.

The sun here describes an individual who is particularly clever in meeting emergencies, or rising to a situation; who exalts efficiency and conformity in every aspect and is in consequence very prone to worry. The beginner has had an example of this fretful and critical temperament in Woodrow Wilson, and will have another case of a more superficially volatile sort in Louis Pasteur. Capricorn as a factor in appearance tends towards a slender body, medium to tall, with the narrow jaw of the goat, a distinctly intellectual head formation, the high cheekbones occasionally giving a very round face; and with small, piercing eyes on the whole, together with a frequent but false suggestion of frailty.

AQUARIUS

The sun is in Aquarius from January 20th through February 18th. This is the falling away of the winter depths of experience, or the time for developing inspiration and desires, and it makes Aquarius the sign of perspective. The symbol is the water-carrier, represented by the waves on the ground as the liquid spills from the jar on his shoulder, and expressing the natural overflow of all life once the inner reservoirs are filled. Aquarius in any chart will show a native's capacity for the preservation of rights and traditions. In the "heavenly man" the sign indicates the blood circulation in general and also the ankles. It therefore reveals a native's ability to put himself into any and every function of individual or social experience, but yet to remain conventional, detached and largely unchanged in the process.

The sun here describes an individual who is doggedly optimistic, and inclined to depend on the cooperation of others; who is gregarious even to the point of concealing his own dogmatic opinions. The beginner has had an excellent example of this type, with its extraordinary difficulty in meeting life on any pliable basis, in Havelock Ellis, and will have two other cases in Lord Byron and General "Chinese" Gordon. Aquarius as a factor in appearance tends towards well-set, filled-out and strong people, generally above medium stature, with a long but very square face, and often with delicate features and a lovely regularity of form; sometimes with a bushy distinguished appearance.

PISCES

♓

The sun is in Pisces from February 19th through March 20th. This is the rising anticipation of spring, or is the time for marshalling ideals and capitalizing on the common faith of men, and it makes Pisces the sign of poetic appreciation. The symbol is the fishes, represented by two curved lines with a stroke to suggest them as they lie bound together facing in opposite directions, and expressing the effort of all life to reach out continually into new or more wonderful experience on every side. Pisces in any chart will show a native's capacity for reflection and rationalizing. In the "heavenly man" the sign indicates the feet. It therefore reveals the fundamental "stand," as well as the poetic gracefulness, by which a native establishes his place among his fellows.

The sun here describes an individual who is always seeking the poetry or hidden meaning in life, or trying to draw out the best in others; who is able to maintain his own point of view under the most diverse circumstances, but is consistently emotional in his efforts to do so. The beginner has had an example of this highly Quixotic temperament in Richard Burton, and an illustration beyond the scope of the book is found in George Washington. Pisces as a factor in appearance tends toward a bodily delicacy which produces either grace or awkwardness, usually of medium stature, with features apt to be round, and with full, prominent eyes apt to show either great depth or watery uncertainty.

Chapter Five

THE MEANING OF THE CROSS

THE beginner is now ready to look at the horoscope in its usual form, and to complete his knowledge of the minimum essentials in horoscopic interpretation. He has gained a general sense of the whole chart by his preliminary examination of exceptional cases. These included hemisphere emphasis on the one hand, and the reverse hemisphere-emphasis of singleton planets on the other. In the meanwhile he has acquired a simple, correct and basic knowledge of the twelve houses, the ten planets and the twelve signs; and this he should review, over and over again, until he is sure of every detail of it in his own mind.

The example chart is Elbert Hubbard, the "sage of East Aurora" and a unique and stimulating literary figure, widely known in America at the turn of the twentieth century. The beginner will notice an east singleton Mars in the twelfth house. This is enlightening because of the degree to which this native carved out his own destiny (the eastern hemisphere-emphasis) by means of his own initiative (the Mars emphasis) and the use of the hidden resources in his own personality (the twelfth house emphasis).

As a matter of fact, the influence of the Mars initiative is so direct in Elbert Hubbard's life that a first house position might seem more correct than the twelfth house place which is given. Here is where it becomes necessary for the beginner to concern himself with the degrees and minutes of the signs. Actually

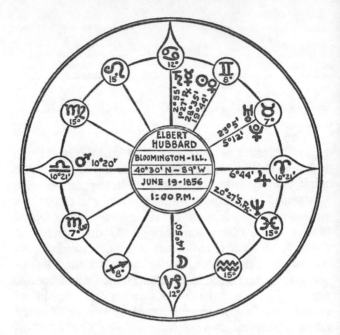

Mars is within a single minute of the cusp, and so its position is probably in the first house after all. This means that if Elbert Hubbard were born only five or ten seconds earlier, or if that much of an error in time had been made in recording his birth, or in casting this chart, or in correcting it, the place of Mars by house would be different. For reasons of this sort it is customary to allow a degree or so, perhaps up to five, in judging whether a planet is on one or another side of a line.

The skilled astrologer will usually make whatever changes are necessary to bring a horoscope into exact conformity with the known facts of a given life, and this is the highly specialized "rectification" which comes with years of practice. It is a matter which need never disturb the beginner if he will remember that few charts have been calculated to a high accuracy in minutes, and that birth times are seldom known to a closer point than the nearest five-minute or quarter-hour interval. He can always make reasonable allowances, as he has already been taught to do. In the meanwhile, however, he will see that he must give real attention to the sign positions, both of planets and house cusps, in definite degrees.

Any circle consists of 360 degrees, and hence a sign as a twelfth of a whole circle must consist of thirty degrees. Each house cusp is shown in the degrees of the zodiac to which it corresponds, hence it may be said that a planet is actually seen or written in the house where it is placed, whereas its position in the sign is shown by the degrees as these are written next to the planet's symbol. In older charts the nearest even degree is usually shown, but in modern practice it is customary to show both degrees and minutes for the planets, and usually for the first and seventh houses also. There are sixty minutes in a degree, and these are not the same "minutes" which divide the hour of time. The symbol for degree is (°) and for minute (′). The symbol for hour is (h) and for its minutes (m). The beginner must be sure to note that the degrees of the zodiac run counterclockwise around the circle, and it may help him to realize at the start that the degree which is Aries 30° is also Taurus 0°, and so on, depending on the point of view at a given time.

A further "look" at the Elbert Hubbard chart will show that four of the planets are near the major south cusp. Saturn is at Cancer 2°55′, which is within a fraction over nine degrees of the cusp at Cancer 12°, and Mercury is a little over a degree farther away at Cancer 1°27′. The sun, at Gemini 28°35′, is within thirteen odd degrees of the cusp, since the 1°25′ in Gemini, added to the twelve degrees in Cancer, makes the exact distance 13°25′. Venus, at Gemini 19°44′, measured in the same fashion, is a little over twenty-two degrees away.

The beginner should be very careful at this point to make sure he understands how distance around the circle is measured in signs and degrees. He should remember the normal order of the signs, seeing clearly how each represents a successive thirty degrees in the whole zodiac circle. He should be able to compute the distance with equal ease counterclockwise or clockwise.

The moon lies almost directly opposite these four planets at the south, a little less than three degrees from the major north cusp. Mars is at the easternmost point of the chart, exactly on the first house cusp, as has been indicated. Jupiter is over at the west angle, less than four degrees from an exact position on the seventh cusp. Pluto is some twenty-five degrees south from this seventh cusp, and Uranus is not quite eighteen degrees farther. Neptune is within a little less than twenty degrees on the northern side. Thus four planets are clustered closely at the south angle, and four are lying not quite as closely at the west. Both the other angles are emphasized by the very close proximity of single planets. This situation in the chart is the astrological configuration known as an "x-cross."

The pattern of the planets here is remarkable in this particular instance for the degree to which they cling to the cusps of the angular houses. They provide a sort of symbolical "crucifixion," or an exceptional case in which the native in a sense is mounted on a "cross" of special strains and stresses. The career of Elbert Hubbard is an excellent dramatization of this unusual emphasis by the house angles, since he consistently felt himself to be in complete rebellion against the existing order of things. His sophisticated attitude gave voice to America's growing protest against mid-Victorian artificiality. The current superficial morality was often a real "crucifixion" of the creative spirit. Hubbard was strikingly sensitive to this shallow sense of values, as is shown by his chart. His Roycroft enterprises at East

Aurora, New York, became an expression of every soul's necessity to break the shackles of an uninteresting existence.

The Aspects

The astrological cross indicates the intensification of this "necessity" in an individual native's case, and it now introduces the beginner to the factor of "aspects" in horoscope interpretation. If he will look at the Hubbard chart again, he will see that Mars and Jupiter are opposite each other by less than four degrees of exactness. In other words, if Jupiter were in Aries 10°20′, that is, 3°36′ farther along, or if Mars were in Libra 6°44′, that is, 3°36′ back of its present place, these two would be directly across from each other on the circle. This state of relation is known as "opposition," and it exists when any two planets are reasonably close to points opposite from each other in this way.

What is "reasonable" depends on practice and opinion. It might be well for the beginner to consider a deviation from exactness of more than 10° as no aspect at all. Many astrologers, however, allow 12°30′ if the moon is a participant in a given aspect, and 17° if the sun is concerned. The allowable deviation of an aspect from exactness is known as the "orb," or "orb of influence," of the planets involved.

Looking further in the example horoscope, it will be observed that the moon is in opposition to Saturn, Mercury and the sun, but not to Venus, according to the extreme extent of orb suggested. Mercury by itself would not be in aspect to the moon here, since the orb is 13°23′, and the moon only permits an extreme orb of 12°30′, but the sun's opposition by less than the 17° allowed carries Mercury into the opposition with it, since Mercury is between the sun and Saturn. This means that there are four oppositions in the chart.

The meaning of an opposition is best approached by going back to the difference between "east" and "west," or "south" and "north." These directions of the compass, first of all, stand contrary to each other; and an opposition is a state of affairs in which two planets, brought to points like east and west, or north and south, likewise stand contrary to each other. Their "contrariety" is not that they cancel each other in any way, since this would violate the principle that nothing properly viewed in a horoscope will contradict anything else determined from the chart, but rather that they challenge each other to an activity of a broader sort. There is at once a tendency to do nothing, and to feel a very great necessity to do something. Superficially the opposition suggests a man who wants to go into both an *à la carte* and a *table d'hôte* restaurant, but who like Buridan's ass cannot make up his mind which, and so goes in neither until some agony of indecision gives birth to a better and single "wanting." The opposition aspect always strengthens the native's awareness of a need to act, together with an accompanying sensitiveness to every difficulty involved in making the decision to act.

Elbert Hubbard had great energy under Mars, but his expansive ideas under Jupiter, in opposition to Mars, kept him interested in too many directions. He was never able to build anything more than the relatively local enterprise which gradually disintegrated after his death on the Lusitania. His feelings and great warm public sympathy, under his moon, were continually involved with his sensitiveness to the motives of others under Saturn, as well as with the working of his own mind under Mercury and with his desire to achieve something of enduring worth under the sun; the three planets in opposition to his moon. Thus when he permitted the New York Central Railroad to put out his *Message to Garcia* on a commercial scale, and decided to be "the Voice of American Business," it is a question whether his really creative conception of his own rôle had not become confused to the point where he never again was able to give real inner direction to his own efforts.

Oppositions are usually accounted "bad" in their influence, as is illustrated in Elbert Hubbard's case by the curious turn in his fate. He put commercial business behind him after a considerable success and then, when William Morris awakened him to the possibilities of genuine craftsmanship in the book printing and binding arts, he ended with what from any fair perspective was only another equally successful commercial enterprise. The greater possibilities were lost for the reason already pointed out.

Yet oppositions from another point of view are also "good." It cannot be forgotten that Elbert Hubbard was very successful in both major chapters of his life, according to all the standards by which men ordinarily judge "success," and that his important oppositions had a large part in such a consummation. In other words his "interest in many directions" made him alert to everything going on around him, and his "involved feelings" took the form of a very practical imagination. What is more, his oppositions might have helped him even further. Had he been able to hold to his deeper call, revealing the inadequacies of his generation and showing men how they were in fact "crucified" by the very superficiality of their living, he would have been true to the higher genius of his chart, as this is shown in the basic x-cross. He might then have gone far in a different way, to leave a truly imperishable name behind him.

The Conjunction and Square

Two other "aspects" can now be introduced. First, the "conjunction" is where two or more planets are within "orb" of the same place in the zodiac. A conjunction means that the activities ruled by these planets will operate in definite cooperation with each other. As in the case of the opposition, this is for better or worse.

Elbert Hubbard's Mercury is in conjunction with Saturn; hence his mind and sensitiveness are indissolubly linked. On the one hand he has great insight, but on the other he is at times merely the "wit"; and this often made it hard for others to take him as more than superficially clever or personally delightful. The sun, his will, is also in conjunction with both these planets, so that his driving ambition is all caught up in this same state of affairs, making him unreasonable and even petty when he cannot dominate a situation. In addition, Venus is in conjunction with the sun, so that his satisfactions are involved also, and his happiness is left dependent on the degree to which he can establish the depth of achievement for which Saturn calls. Elbert Hubbard suffers for being less than that of which he is capable.

The "square" aspect is an altogether different sort of relation from anything brought to the beginner's attention thus far. It represents what is almost a side-issue in the consideration, and this is almost exactly its nature as an aspect. In other words, it reveals a tendency to get off into side issues, by one way of explaining it, or it is more accurately a situation when various activities of life are a mutual difficulty to each other, leading to a joint accomplishment that would not be possible to either activity alone; and yet often failing to reach any state of accomplishment and so ending with mere frustration and destructive results.

The aspect is the sort of relation that would exist between the east (or west) point of one hemisphere line, and the south (or north) point of the other. These two lines create the hemispheres with which the beginner started his study. The operation of a square is not unlike what would happen if some situation were worked out as an east-west matter, for example, and then a south-north consideration were to be brought in rather suddenly. A man (first house) and his enemy (seventh) might start on the settlement of their differences when the arm of the government (tenth house) or the hysteria of the families of either or both (fourth) might come on the scene and thoroughly upset the progress of the struggle. However, the intervention of the one class of affairs in the other might work out a much better solution than otherwise possible. The law could offer court arbitration as a peaceful substitute for a duel, and the woman's influence out of the home might change hatred into friendliness. The whole point, of course, is that the square is the great indication in astrology of the bringing of affairs to a point where general revision and new consideration are a necessity in the matter.

The moon in Elbert Hubbard's chart is within 5° of an exact square to Mars. His feelings have a tendency to stimulate his initiative in unimportant matters, on the one hand, and his actual move in starting anything is very apt to stir up some sort of alien emotional response or to confuse the direction of his energy, on the other. This was shown in the great unpredictability of his actions as administrator of affairs of East Aurora. Some transient impulse (the moon) would upset his normal activities (Mars), and the same sort of thing operated also in the square relations of moon and Jupiter, and of both Mars and Jupiter with Saturn, Mercury and the sun.

Hubbard's colorful, dramatic and almost erratic career can be traced out through the various combinations of these squares. Like the opposition, they are usually accounted "bad," but their "good" is also evident. They made him an outstanding personality, even if they had no chance to contribute to any superlatively high achievement. The square at its best is an aspect of "construction" or "building." The deflection of influences is illustrated here in more or less destructive cross-purposes, but it will also serve to distribute things into some desired pattern. The stresses and strains of life may be set to the task of supporting a very worthy structure of effort. One purpose of the horoscope is to determine how this can be done in any particular case.

The Quadratures

The beginner has been helped over the first hurdle of the aspects by the use of an example chart in which all the planets are fairly close to the lines of the angular houses, and where for the most part they lie in a basic pattern of opposition, square and conjunction relationships. The relationships have been evident to the eye because the east-west cusps are within less than a 2° deviation from a perpendicular to the south-north cusps. Horoscopes of this convenient sort, however, are not at all common in astrology. The young astrologer will never dare trust the lines of the house-cusps for revealing the aspects among the planets. Consequently, at this point, he must learn the pairs of opposites among the signs as a first step towards a better method for recognizing the planetary relations.

Aries	is opposite	Libra
Taurus	is opposite	Scorpio
Gemini	is opposite	Sagittarius
Cancer	is opposite	Capricorn
Leo	is opposite	Aquarius
Virgo	is opposite	Pisces

He then proceeds to the naturally square relations among the signs, which establishes them in groups of four. These are the "quadratures." In Elbert Hubbard's chart the signs on the four angular houses are Aries at the west, Cancer at the south, Libra at the east and Capricorn at the north, or the group known as the "cardinal signs"; the first or most important quadrature. The cardinal signs have a very general correspondence to the angular houses.

In similar but very superficial correspondence to the succedent houses, and here placed on the succedent cusps, or the eighth, eleventh, second and fifth houses in that order, are the "fixed signs," Taurus, Leo, Scorpio and Aquarius. In like correspondence to the cadent houses, and placed on the cadent cusps in Hubbard's chart, or the ninth, twelfth, third and sixth, are the "common signs," Gemini, Virgo, Sagittarius and Pisces.

Except when the orb of an aspect permits it to be made across the line of a sign, illustrated in Elbert Hubbard's case by the sun (near the end of a common sign) square to Jupiter (near the beginning of a cardinal sign), planets in aspect and placed in the same quadrature are conjunction, square or opposition to each other. Knowledge of this fact will spare the student many embarrassing mistakes in the horoscopes where the cusps of the houses might make the planets seem to be in a relation quite different from their actual situation.

The T-Cross

The principal significance of quadrature is revealed in its emphasis by the "cosmic cross" pattern, of which Elbert Hubbard is the x-cross or the more unusual example. The t-cross form is far more common in practice. This is what would appear in Elbert Hubbard's chart if the moon, for example, were in Libra 14° instead of Capricorn 14°, or if Jupiter, Mars or the group at the beginning line of Cancer were similarly found at one of the other legs of the cross; or if any at any one leg had been found outside the square and opposition pattern. It is a stronger and a much more favorable indication on the whole. The reason is that the lack of a fourth leg in the cross prevents the wide diffusion of energies usually indicated by the "x" form, and dramatically illustrated in Hubbard's career.

Cardinal-Sign Emphasis

The "cardinal cross" is the basic type of the three. The example chart is Annie Besant, a famous leader among the Theosophists, and one of the most brilliant women produced by modern England.

The cosmic cross of the "t" pattern gives an overbalanced emphasis of the life according to the quadrature in which it is found. The excess activity is principally directed toward the point of the "short leg," or is revealed by the planet which has only the square or "construction" aspects. In Mrs. Besant's case this is Jupiter, which has exceptionally close squares of less than 2° to Mercury, or mind, and to Uranus, or independence. Thus her enthusiasm is shown as the foundation of her achievements. It is to be noticed that her moon, sun, Venus and Pluto are also included in this cross configuration, so that seven out of ten planets contribute to the tremendous focal power of Jupiter in her house of ultimate ends. Theosophy gave her the definitely all-inclusive or absolute ordering of life which her fourth house required, and the chance to show her rebuilding talent for which Cancer called. Jupiter gave her an organizing leadership on the pattern of Bismarck, in distinction from the more superficial pioneering of Mars, and she eventually made herself Theosophy's best known exponent.

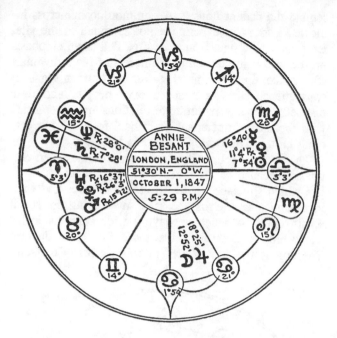

A cardinal cosmic-cross indicates a life fundamentally concerned with the critical or vital issues of human experience. If the person is important enough, his career is irrevocably linked with the broad crises of a nation, a movement or an age. Annie Besant came to a position of leadership in Theosophy when it was torn by many dissentions. It has already been seen how Elbert Hubbard, with an x-cross in this cardinal quadrature, became an outstanding voice in the cultural crisis of the nineties, or the general rebellion against mid-Victorian conservatism.

Common-Sign Emphasis

The common signs are the ones which support or underlie the cardinal group, and in that respect they resemble the cadent houses. A common cosmic-cross indicates a focus of experience not so much in the vital issues as in the background of life. This is an emphasis on the well-being or common interest of the individuals who make up the general culture. Common signs in consequence show a concern over people, and over distinctly personal or intimate relationships, in contrast with the more impersonal or critical focus of the cardinal group. The example chart is Emerson.

This is an excellent illustration of common sign emphasis, because of the wide spirit of practical humanism which Emerson voiced in all his lectures and writings, and because of the new awakening in social sensitiveness to which he gave a wide stimulus in his friendships and through his more indirect influence. The sun is the key planet in this t-cross. Emerson's

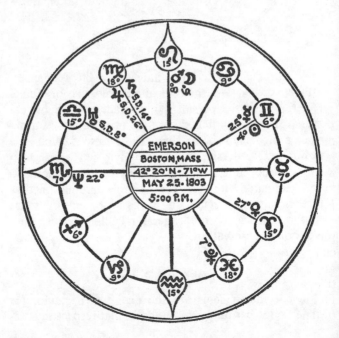

dynamic concept of life revealed a limitless opportunity to all men, through the sun's place in the seventh house, and an unquenchable inner enthusiasm, through the planet's position in Gemini. The chart is interestingly akin to those of Shakespeare and Sir William Hamilton because the cross is made possible by Pluto's discovery in 1930. Emerson's contribution was not only in advance of his own age, but also beyond his own understanding of its full significance in his own lifetime.

If a person is important enough, a common cross irrevocably links him with the living personality of a nation, a movement or an age. Emerson was unquestionably a central figure in the stirring towards a reconstitution of American life which Elbert Hubbard dramatized somewhat differently at its point of great crisis under the pattern of a cardinal sign emphasis. The contrast between these men affords valuable and additional light on the nature of both quadratures.

Fixed-Sign Emphasis

The fixed signs are the ones which order the cardinal group, reaching out ahead of them on the analogy of the succedent houses. This means a focus of interest in patterns and principles, or in more abstract or remote possibilities. A fixed cosmic-cross indicates a fundamental concern with ideas, or with the intangible and "value" side of life. The example chart is the elder J. P. Morgan.

This is an excellent illustration of fixed sign emphasis because Morgan centered his career in the financial realm, where ideas and values are manipulated, and where transactions are made out of such intangible things as stocks, bonds and the like. Saturn is the key planet in this horoscope, so that the focus of the life is through its sensitiveness. This becomes the financier's

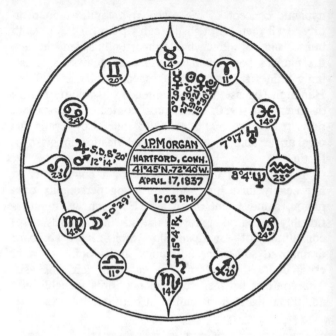

very special "instinct" for dealing with intangibles. Saturn lies in the fourth house, accentuating his concern over such established assets as the capital investments, plants and equipment of a corporation, and in Scorpio, which indicate his outstanding capacity for creating financial and business structures in American society.

If a person is important enough, a fixed cross irrevocably links him with the establishment of the values, or the patterns of motives and belief, in a nation, a movement or an age. Morgan, more than any other figure, has remained the ideal type of American financial genius. He represents the whole modern concept of sheer financial power, or economic exploitation. Another man may represent a finer turn in the events which through Emerson and Hubbard, typically at least, marked the rise of a strictly American everyday philosophy, but in any case the elder Morgan's life excellently illustrates the real nature of a fixed-sign emphasis.

Summary

In summary, what has the beginner learned in this fifth chapter? He has been introduced to the degrees of the zodiac by which position in the signs is indicated. He has been shown how to use these in determining the aspects; specifically the oppositions, conjunctions and squares. He has been told how to apply the test of "orb," or to find whether an aspect is close enough to have any influence.

He has been given the chart of Elbert Hubbard in the usual form. He has seen through this example how life is patterned in the symbolism of the horoscope, and how the native becomes thwarted as well as stimulated or aided by the conditions of his experience. He has been shown the difference in meaning among the three aspects so far presented, and it has been pointed out how these aspects may work for good or bad, depending on the native's direction of his own life.

He has been introduced to astrological quadrature. He has learned that cardinal signs have principal correspondence to the critical issues in life, common signs to the personal affairs of people, and fixed signs to the relations and activities of ideas in both individual and group situations.

Chapter Six

THE MEANING OF THE TRIANGLE

THE horoscope not only reveals the stresses and strains in experience, through the relations set up by the "cross" in the circle, but also the cooperation which the triangle similarly indicates and symbolizes. The triangle is the geometrical figure by which points are emphasized as they tend to help rather than oppose or block each other. The triangle divides the circle of the astrological chart "around" the quarter points; it sets up relationships independent of the quarter points, or the squares and oppositions which always indicate an essential difficulty.

The classification of the signs by quadrature has disclosed the square and opposition relationship between the planets, subject of course to the orbs of influence. A further classification by "triplicity," so called because there are three signs in each grouping, will provide the similar indication of a possible triangle relation. Astrologers term this relation a "trine" aspect. It is measured in the same way as the others, and is accepted according to the same planetary orbs.

Parenthetically, the planets in the same triplicity may be in conjunction rather than trine. Also it is necessary to remember that any aspect may be formed across the lines of a sign when the planets are near either edge.

The easiest way to learn the triplicities, as well as the significance of the trine aspect, is through the special emphasis given by a configuration known to as-

trologers as a "grand trine." This is an arrangement
of the planets around the circle so that two of them,
trine to each other, are both trine to a third on the
other side of the circle. The first example horoscope
for the grand trine is Mahatma Gandhi.

If an equal-sided triangle is inscribed in the zodiac
here, with one point at Aries 18°27', or at the position
of Gandhi's Neptune, the two other points will be
found at the same degree and minute of Leo and Sagittarius. These three signs constitute the "fire" triplicity.
Since Gandhi has his moon within 1°46' of Neptune's
trine point in Leo, his Saturn within 6°5' of this same
trine point in Sagittarius, and his moon and Saturn also
within 7°51' of an exact trine to each other, these three
planets constitute a grand trine.

The grand trine in Gandhi's horoscope supplements
a much stronger cosmic-cross in fixed signs. This latter

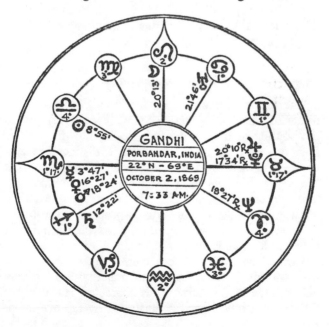

pattern indicates that the mahatma lives in a world of potentialities. It reveals his task in establishing values or dealing with motives, and links him with J. P. Morgan. This parallel to the American financier's case gives the beginner a foundation for understanding the career of the East Indian saint, and also presents another illustration of the fact that the meaning derived from any one part of the horoscope will never properly contradict or modify that derived from any other. Whatever the fire grand-trine signifies will be true in all instances, irrespective of what else the chart may reveal.

A triplicity consists of one sign from each of the three quadratures, just as the quadratures in turn include one from each of the four triplicities. This can be seen clearly in the table on page 103. The cardinal or most important quadrature sign is the key member in every triplicity. It gives the triplicity its meaning through the relationship set up with the four seasonal points of the zodiac circle; i.e., the spring and autumn equinoxes and the summer and winter solstices.

Fire-Sign Emphasis

The spring equinox is the "fire" point because it indicates the beginning phase of experience. It represents the pouring of life, or the fire of self, into the various functions of nature. A chart with a distinct fire emphasis is marked by some outstanding effort to put this life-giving spirit into whatever affairs are of momentary concern. Gandhi's chart is an excellent example because his leadership in India is primarily "spiritual," or fire-like. He is far more a religious than a political figure in his manifestation of this high exaltation.

Horoscopes with either a cosmic cross or a grand trine will always indicate an individual with some particular intensified quality in his character. He may put this to great advantage, as illustrated by the mahatma, or he may equally be lost in a broad diffusion of his own energies. The general tendency of the grand trine, like the x-cross in the quadratures, is towards the scattering temperament. In consequence, the older astrologers always classify it as "bad," although trines otherwise are taken as the very extreme of "good." In Gandhi's case, in support of this tradition, it may be noticed that despite all his achievement under the dynamic idealism of his fixed cross, he has consistent difficulty in consolidating his gains.

In the cosmic cross of the "t" variety there is always a planet at the short "leg," to be taken as the focal one of the group, but in a grand trine the determination of a focal planet must depend on other factors. The cardinal sign is primary in a triplicity's meaning, but not necessarily in its functioning. Gandhi's chart is helpful to the beginner because the moon lies in both the grand trine and the cosmic cross. This alone would make it focal for the grand trine, but in addition it is placed at the short leg of the cross, greatly increasing its influence in both patterns. The result is that Gandhi's career, focused under the moon, is centered in his feelings, or his warmth of relations with others. He is very like Sir Richard Burton in this one detail. A moon emphasis calls for a public life, or a broad humanitarian interest of some sort. With this planet in the tenth house, the necessity for a rather spectacular career is indicated. The sign Leo, which contains the moon, shows how Gandhi must dramatize his high ideals on every occasion.

The other planets in the grand trine complete the picture of his fire emphasis. Neptune in Aries indicates the sense of social obligation which gives Gandhi his deep motivation, or the practical direction of his activity, and its place in the sixth house accounts for his persisting desire to serve his fellows, and enlist their services for his cause. Saturn or his sensitiveness lies in Sagittarius, and this indicates a real distributive or executive ability in his adjustment of his vision to realities. The place of this planet in his second house reveals his essentially spiritual resources in meeting the problems of his long crusade.

If the beginner has any difficulty at this point in following these delineations of the example horoscopes, or in understanding the source of the observations made, it will repay him richly to go back and review the information already given in connection with the meaning of the houses, planets and signs in order. There is much to be added by way of new details in interpretation, and hopeless confusion will be the only result when progress is crowded, or when the mind is asked to build on incomplete foundations.

The planets in any grand trine are cooperatively linked in a special manifestation of the basic quality which each triplicity represents, and in the mahatma's horoscope his feelings, his sensitiveness to experience, and his obligation to the race or society as a whole are all three continually fused together in the "fire" or inspiration of his great work. The moon, Saturn and Neptune are each what they are on their own account, and together they are also something more.

A single trine blends its members together in the same fashion, but not in any special exaggeration of the given triplicity as in the grand trine. The manifestation of the single trine is more obvious in the terms of a general cooperation. This is active through the phase of life which the planets in trine will represent jointly. Thus the fire trine of Mars and Venus in the horoscope of J. P. Morgan, where no grand trine is found, and taking this one out of his several trines from Aries to Leo, gives him an extraordinary facility for picking up (Mars) and putting down (Venus) the various interests with which he dealt. This single trine shows how largely his power was based on a complete freedom of outer action, so that he could always move in quick response to the inner or "idea" pattern established by his fixed cosmic-cross.

Lord Byron, the modern romantic poet, is the convenient example chart for the grand trine in "air."

Air-Sign Emphasis

Libra is the sign of the autumnal equinox, expressing the definite turn of life to its inner or ideal values, and the grand trine in air is an overemphasis of this effort to bring everything to a quick harvest. Neptune in Libra, at this cardinal point in Byron's horoscope, provides a parallel to Gandhi's case, where Neptune was in the cardinal sign of the fire triplicity. This shows how effectively the dynamic compulsion felt by

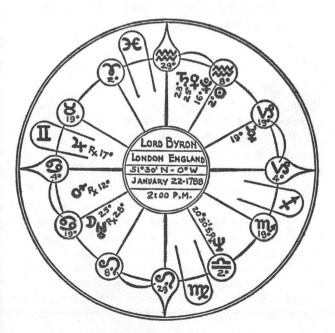

both of them has arisen in their sense of current social limitation on human lives, and in their appreciation of the need to do something about it. Gandhi's fire emphasis led him to direct action, whereas the air focus led Byron to an essentially intellectual attack. Here is one root distinction between fire and air, and it is dramatized to the last detail by the difference in the achievement of these two men.

Lord Byron's grand trine is completed by three planets in Aquarius and Jupiter in Gemini, so that Libra and these two signs constitute the triplicity. Venus, taking one of the three in Aquarius, and Jupiter reveal respectively his keen desire to break up an old order of things, or to establish a better basis of human satisfactions, and his determination to expand this effort in new directions. They give a rather superficial indication in contrast with the deeper stirrings shown by the moon and Saturn in Gandhi's chart.

Intercepted Signs

The beginner now encounters another factor in astrology. If he will turn back to the chart of Annie Besant, comparing it with Byron's, he will notice in both that the twelfth and sixth houses stretch across more than 30° of the zodiac. This may happen quite commonly to any pair of the houses, and it is a situation that can now be observed in seven of the earlier charts even as they are given in their simplified form.

The explanation begins with the fact that the first house cusp is established by the horizon, and the horizon must necessarily tilt up towards the north or down towards the south whenever a person is born anywhere except at the equator. It is a complication to which a second must be added. The whole circle of the houses is tilted away from the circle of the signs permanently, and for quite another reason. Here is the astronomical fact which causes the difference between summer and winter. However, the beginner only needs to understand all this in the most general way; he will find it of no particular value to master the celestial mechanics involved, except for very specialized work.

As a result of these two complications, whenever the "ascendant" or first-house cusp of a horoscope is away from either Aries or Libra, the houses in general, in the terms of their indication by signs and degrees of the zodiac, will become more and more irregular as the birth in turn takes place increasingly towards the north or south poles on the earth's surface. If a house is elongated in this way, again in terms of the zodiacal signs and degrees on the cusps that bound it, a sign may often lie between the cusps on each side. In such a case the sign fails to have any primary relationship with any house, and it is said to be "intercepted." When this happens, any planets contained in the sign are also said to be "intercepted."

Interception is regarded as an indication of weakness. It means that a planet's activity is more subjective, or psychological. In consequence, the activities it rules are more difficult to identify on the one hand, and to subject to conscious direction on the other. Thus the intercepted situation of Jupiter in Lord Byron's horoscope is a testimony against its primary influence, a point of value in determining which of the grand-trine planets is to be taken as focal.

Retrogradation

Again, the beginner will note that Jupiter's symbol is marked with a special "R," and by turning back he will see that Saturn is marked this way in J. P. Morgan's chart, Mercury and Neptune in Elbert Hubbard's chart, Jupiter, Neptune and Pluto in Gandhi's, and a total of six planets in Annie Besant's; together with three others in the present example. The "R" indicates that a planet is "retrograde" or that, as its motion is seen from the earth, it is slipping backwards or moving clockwise in the heavens.

The phenomenon of retrogradation is due to the fact that the earth's motion in its own path, at a time when the angle of observation permits, causes the planet to be overtaken momentarily. It is the same proposition, in effect, as when a faster train, passing a slower, makes the latter seem to be backing. All the planets other than the sun and moon are retrograde at fairly regular intervals. The meaning is much the same as interception. The planet's activity to some extent is turned around, or is brought to indicate a primarily reflexive, subjective or psychological experience.

Byron's Jupiter therefore, on two counts of weakness, is rejected as a possible focal planet in the grand trine. Moreover, it is in a cadent house in comparison with Neptune in a succedent one. This is important because angular position is stronger than succedent and succedent is stronger than cadent. By the same token, cardinal position is stronger than fixed or common; and of these latter the common position is taken as the stronger because it is more concerned with human values. This holds despite the fact that common signs have a superficial correspondence to cadent houses, and it is a detail of astrological practice that sometimes leads to considerable confusion.

The beginner may find it hard about this time to keep this new astrological vocabulary straight in mind, especially in view of the rapidity with which it must be expanded. The glossary in the back of the book should now serve him well. He will do much better looking up the words, if necessary over and over, than trying to force them all into his memory before they have any real or living meaning for him. This procedure will provide a species of continuous review for him, and review is one of the genuinely royal roads to knowledge.

Venus in Byron's chart, while neither intercepted nor retrograde, is cadent like Jupiter, a count against its dominance. Also, it is in a fixed sign in comparison with the common placing of Jupiter and the cardinal position of Neptune, a second adverse testimony to its basic importance. In view of this, and the relative weakness of Jupiter, Neptune must be taken as the focal planet in this grand trine, and hence as the fundamental clue to Lord Byron's life.

The same indication is given, in striking confirmation of these deductions, by the fact that Neptune is placed on the short leg of a cardinal t-cross. This indicates the great extent to which the poet was involved in the issues of his day. The fact that Neptune is in the fifth house suggests that Byron centered his life activity in some form of self-expression or artistic effort, such as his poetry, and the fact that it is in Libra indicates that he had to stimulate human experience wherever he went, as is shown by his romantic idealism in general and by his efforts for Greek independence in particular.

Many readers will have no idea what is meant by the phrase "efforts for Greek independence." They simply will not know that Byron took any actual part in the revolt of the Greeks against the Turks, or that he actually gave his life to the cause. This possibility points to the great value resulting from at least a brief survey of each example life, in connection with the study of the text; and especially when the beginner turns to a further analysis of these charts for practice in delineation.

Water-Sign Emphasis

Goethe, known for the universal quality of his genius, is the example chart of the summer triplicity, and a particularly apt one because "water" is a symbol of practical universality, and a grand trine in that triplicity will call for a particularly intensive struggle for universal harmony.

Again Neptune lies in the cardinal sign of the given triplicity, which here is Cancer; and again a given career arises in protest against the unnecessary compulsions on human life. Saturn in Scorpio and the moon in Pisces complete the grand trine. The three signs are thus identified as the water group. In estimating the focal planet along the lines laid down in the preceding cases, it will be observed that Saturn is cadent and

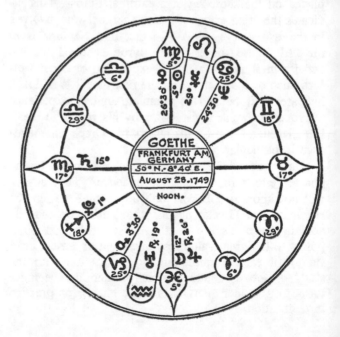

GOETHE
FRANKFURT AM GERMANY
50° N. 8° 40' E.
AUGUST 28, 1749
NOON.

fixed in its situation, hence eliminated at once from consideration. The moon is angular, and in a common sign. While it participates in a curiously loose cosmic-cross, this brings diffusion rather than strength to Goethe's life, and the moon does not lie at the focal leg, so that the relation is of no present consequence. Neptune is succedent by house, and cardinal by sign, just about balancing the angular-common placing of the moon.

However, Neptune is given a particular strengthening by Venus, a point to be explained immediately. The moon and Saturn are each strengthened in this same way, but in neither case with the same close degree of relation and importance which marks the Neptune-Venus cooperation. Thus Neptune becomes the key to Goethe's chart. The planet, which indicates the extreme sense of social obligation in any life, is here found in the self-centered sign Cancer, giving every benefit from Cancer's emphasis on inner growth, and in the eighth house, where the rulership of regeneration, self-reconstitution and rediscovery is a clear indication of the special creative quality which Goethe exhibited in writing *Faust*.

The Sextile

Reference has been made to the "particular strengthening" which Venus gives to Neptune in Goethe's chart. This introduces the beginner to the sextile, or the last of five major aspects. The sextile is quite accurately a "half-trine," and its indication is the trine's cooperation in a lesser degree, or in a relationship of simple "assistance." It is called a "sextile" because it is a sixth instead of a third of a circle. Its significance follows from the fact that the fire and air elements have a kindred origin at the equinoxial points, somewhat analogous to the east and west house-angles, and that the water and earth triplicities are similarly associated in origin through the summer and winter solstices, on much the same pattern as the complementary relations of the south and north angles.

The nearest earth sign to Cancer is Virgo in one direction and Taurus in the other, and the sextile point of Neptune in either of these would be 24°30′. Venus lies within 2° of this in Virgo, and so forms a very strong sextile. It gives vital assistance to Goethe by equipping him with the power to complete his drama, and its great revelation of the moral compulsion on man. The place of Venus in the tenth house assisted the final and universal recognition of *Faust,* while the situation of Neptune in the eighth house compelled his continual refinement of the poem, and so led to its consequent ultimate perfection.

Earth-Sign Emphasis

One of the most famous of British generals, Charles George Gordon, more familiarly known as "Chinese" Gordon, is the example chart for the winter triplicity. "Earth," as the complementary quality to water's universality, is the greatest possible resort to particular, immediate and practical self-responsibility, and a grand trine here will indicate an overemphasized sensitiveness of this special type.

Neptune again lies in the cardinal sign of the triplicity, which is Capricorn. Mars in Taurus and Saturn in Virgo complete the grand trine, and identify the three signs of the group. Because Saturn is intercepted, retrograde and cadent, Gordon's sensitiveness is entirely a subjective or private affair. From this it might well seem that Saturn is not the focal planet, and its

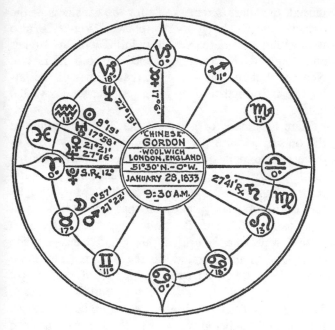

claims would be dismissed at once in a tentative first analysis if it were not an obvious and powerful singleton. There is an exact parallel to the life of Havelock Ellis here, and Saturn cannot be pushed aside.

Mars and Neptune are no better than succedent by house, so that neither has an outstanding house emphasis. The cardinal place of Neptune gives it a precedence over Mars in a fixed sign, but this is not conclusive testimony to its focal importance because it certainly must be possible for a grand trine to have its emphasis through its fixed sign. A further examination of the chart shows that Jupiter and Venus are placed in the water sign between Mars and Neptune in earth. Jupiter is exactly on the sextile point of both;

indeed, the chart is remarkable for the exactness of the aspects among the four key planets. Venus is also well within orb of the sextile point. Therefore Jupiter and Venus give strong assistance to both Mars and Neptune, but in such a fashion that neither of the latter two is strengthened or given prominence above the other.

Here is a mode of judgment that is difficult only at the outset, because it is unfamiliar. When two out of three related points are strengthened equally over the third weaker one, the weakness at this third point becomes the active focus of the matter. More simply, this is the obvious proposition that whatever is most significantly different is most important. The idea is that while the Saturn of this grand trine is made subjective on three counts, in the life of a man who superficially seems an extremely practical person, yet the real emphasis in his life was entirely reflexive. This was especially indicated in his religious fervor, his quixotic temperament, and in the fact that he won his greatest successes when loaned to governments other than his own, or when executing realities that belonged to someone else. The case shows how definitely a horoscope will correct merely surface or "taken for granted" judgments about people.

The singleton Saturn tells the same story as the grand trine focused at the sensitiveness of that planet. From either point of view the assimilative necessity of Virgo, and the stress on service provided by the sixth house, give the true picture of Gordon's life. There is no contradiction of his everyday practicality (the earth grand-trine) in his deeper obligation to conform always to the convenience of others (a hemisphere emphasis in the west).

The focal importance of Saturn is shown further by

its exact-to-the-degree opposition to Jupiter. With its equally exact trines to Neptune and Mars, Saturn builds the whole configuration into a special planetary pattern sometimes known as a "fanhandle." This is an arrangement, adequately described by its name, in which the effect of a singleton planet is practically redoubled. Saturn's influence here fans out through all these other planets.

The Stellium

Of all the common patterns in which the planets will be encountered, only one more has an easily recognizable form. This is the "stellium." Louis Pasteur, French genius in the investigation and control of disease germs, is the example chart.

The stellium is the presence of four or more planets, at least two of them other than the sun, Mercury and Venus, in one house or one sign. It indicates an exceptional emphasis of the life in the terms of the given house or sign. Here the stellium is by both house and sign. The third-house emphasis shows the degree to which Pasteur was able to control the real functioning of his immediate environment, even to the point of locating and controlling microscopic life, while the emphasis of Capricorn indicates the extraordinary creative resource by which he gained his scientific immortality.

Summary

In summary, what has the beginner learned in this sixth chapter? He has been introduced to the "trine" and "sextile" aspects, and to the triplicities or "elements" of fire, air, water and earth. He has seen how

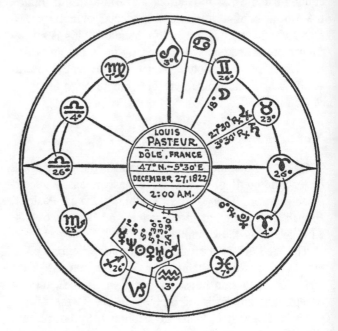

it is possible, on the basis of these distinctions, together with the ones he has had before, to get at the focus of every human activity through the special emphasis given to one or another planet in the chart. He has approached the study of life in terms of its free cooperations, as in contrast with the strains and stresses revealed through the cross and its functions. He has had a further detailed drill in the use of many factors already placed in his possession. In passing, he has encountered the phenomena of "interception" and "retrogression," and has given some attention to their significance in the horoscope.

THE PRINCIPAL ASPECTS

Symbol	Name	Degrees of Separation When Aspect is Exact
☌	Conjunction	0°
⁎	Sextile	60°
□	Square	90°
△	Trine	120°
☍	Opposition	180°

PRINCIPAL OR KEY DESIGNATIONS OF THE SIGNS

Name	Symbol	Rulership	Quadrature	Triplicity
Aries	Ram	Head	Cardinal	Fire
Taurus	Bull	Throat	Fixed	Earth
Gemini	Twins	Lungs, Arms	Common	Air
Cancer	Crab	Stomach	Cardinal	Water
Leo	Lion	Heart	Fixed	Fire
Virgo	Virgin	Intestines	Common	Earth
Libra	Scales	Kidneys	Cardinal	Air
Scorpio	Scorpion	Privates	Fixed	Water
Sagittarius	Archer	Flesh, Thighs	Common	Fire
Capricorn	Goat	Skin, Knees	Cardinal	Earth
Aquarius	Water-carrier	Ankles	Fixed	Air
Pisces	Fishes	Feet	Common	Water

Chapter Seven

THE DETAILS OF INTERPRETATION

THE first step in looking at a horoscope is to get an over-all view. This affords a perspective for the later or more thorough analysis, and it also gives a reasonable check on the accuracy of the chart itself. Thus the sign on the ascendant should be noted, as well as the sign containing the sun, to see whether or not these two signs give an acceptable clue to the native's character, and account for his general appearance. Then the outstanding "focal determinators" should be located.

The major factors in establishing basic patterns have already been described, but it is necessary to consider some other possibilities, together with the order in which the patterns should be taken; and also to learn certain distinctions which give a special weight to some planets over others. The various focal determinators are not to be understood as in any way better or worse than each other, but only as keys to the fundamental difference in human lives. Thus hemisphere emphasis, rather than an aid to success, or a hindrance to it, is merely an indication of the terms on which the success must be won, if it is to be gained at all.

In other words, there are some few things that a tall man can do better than a short one, but these are relatively unimportant in the face of all the potentialities of life. In the same way it makes little difference, comparatively, what the focal determination may be in any given chart. A man born to speak English will find it easier to live among English-speaking people, by and large, but this circumstance does not mean that he will be a better mechanic or a worse tennis player. Focal determination is the way the astrologer gains his first orienting look at a chart, and it reveals the general type of relation by which the native makes his root contact with the life about him. The common determinators are best given in the order of the ease with which they can be recognized by an initial glance, but the listing is in no way a scale of their relative value.

THE DETERMINATORS OF FOCAL EMPHASIS

1. Hemisphere emphasis
2. Singleton planet
3. Cosmic cross
4. Grand trine
5. Stellium
6. Similarity to known type
7. Preponderance
8. Weighted planets

The determinators following the stellium have still to be described. They represent a sharp change in point of view, or a switch from actual planetary patterns to a consideration of various types of relationship, each with its own special characteristics.

"Similarity to known type" is the general likeness of new charts to horoscopes already possessed. It is also the reasonable approach of some new pattern to a more common focal determinator. In any case it means that the mind is given a familiar anchorage. The young astrologer, as he grows in experience, will discover definite types of charts turning up in his work fairly frequently. When he finds that a new individual has a horoscope with a definite resemblance, in one respect or another, to some chart he already has mastered, he has a valuable and correct clue to the new life. The great astrologers of prior ages actually worked this way, since they had no body of accumulated data on which to draw. There were few books, and mostly of little worth.

Preponderance

"Preponderance" is any case when an outstanding number of planets are drawn together in a common situation with definite meaning. This is the widest used and earliest known form of focal determination. Thus the majority of printed horoscope-blanks available for students in recent years are equipped with places to make special tabulations, and so discover what degree of preponderance may exist. While the methods are often unnecessarily cumbersome, they are entirely correct.

The usually recognized forms of "preponderance" are, first, in connection with the angular, succedent and cadent houses. Of the charts in the preceding chapter, the only real case of house preponderance, outside of the Pasteur stellium, is Gandhi, with six planets in angular houses. This testifies to the fact that his whole life must be lived out in public, and in the midst of critical issues. This is equally true of Annie Besant in the fifth chapter, with eight angular planets. In that chapter, by contrast, Elbert Hubbard has seven of his planets in cadent houses, and so has J. P. Morgan. Consequently, both of these men are seen to operate primarily with hidden or deeper factors in life. Hubbard made real traffic out of esthetic appreciation and mid-Victorian inhibitions, while Morgan profited by the new and mysterious entity known as the financial trust, with its use of interlocking directorates and other somewhat dubious devices. In the third chapter, the horoscope of Richard Burton shows eight planets in succedent houses, a fact which gives graphic testimony to his gift for self-expenditure and for expanding every phase of his experience.

The next type of common preponderance is the presence of an overbalancing number of planets in some one quadrature or triplicity. The cosmic cross, grand trine and stellium are the beginning of such a situation, as in the eight earth planets of Pasteur, the seven cardinal planets of Pasteur and Annie Besant, and the six air planets of Lord Byron. However, preponderance only accompanies these major patterns occasionally, and it is interesting to note that J. P. Morgan, with a fixed cross giving the most valuable insight into the focal determination of his horoscope and his life, yet has five planets in fire signs. This is a preponderance which indicates the single-mindedness and self-sufficiency by which he was characterized, despite his fixed cross obsession with broad ideas or intangible values; and once again it is seen how each signification in astrology will hold true in its own case, irrespective of what others may be found.

Weighted Planets

"Weighted planets" are the astrological orientation on which nineteenth century horoscopy preeminently depended. Many of the older books are almost filled with the details of "dignities" and "debilities," or the factors in this weighting. It is sufficient for the present-day beginner to be able to recognize the strength a planet will possess in certain selected cases of preferential position. The simplest type of this is what the older astrologers knew as "accidental dignity." A special example is the singleton, which is an unusually valuable determinator whenever it is found. Of somewhat lesser importance, a planet standing alone near the tenth-house or midheaven cusp, is the "elevated planet" of the horoscope. It has an enhanced influence in the life, and tends to bring honors to the native according to its nature and rulership. By the same token, a planet alone in the first house, or moving ahead of a group of others in that position, is the "rising planet." It reveals a particular strength in the resources of personality, according to its nature and rulership.

The importance of Saturn in Elbert Hubbard's chart, and of the moon in Gandhi's, is greatly enhanced by the fact that these are elevated planets. This position of Mercury in the horoscopes of both J. P. Morgan and "Chinese" Gordon, of the sun in Goethe's, of Saturn in Lord Byron's, and of Mars in Emerson's, give testimony to some rather important facts. Morgan and General Gordon held their places in life as representative of other people, or according to the "messenger" function of their elevated planet. Goethe had to speak for the dignity of all humanity, under the sun's influence, as he did in *Faust*. Both Byron and Hubbard were called to give voice to the broad sensitiveness of the race itself, as has been suggested, each in his special way. The influence of Gandhi's moon has already been indicated at length, as has the pioneer career of Emerson now further revealed by his elevated Mars.

In similar fashion the rising Mars of Byron is testimony to his impulsiveness. Since it is retrograde, it also reveals his anarchistic and introspective attitude. The rising Mercury of Gandhi, by contrast, shows the mahatma's extreme sensitiveness to the situation in which he enacts his prophet's rôle. The rising Pluto of Goethe and General Gordon gives them the characteristic personal "detachment," as well as the typical reaction to remote rather than immediate factors, which is evident in a later century with the discovery of this planet. The rising Mars of Elbert Hubbard places him in special kinship with Lord Byron. The rising and retrograde Uranus of Annie Besant yields a perfect description of her self-willed, introspective independence, and the rising Neptune of Emerson indicates the extent to which he was a true voice of his age.

The other principal type of preferential position among the planets is what the older astrologers called "essential dignity," or advantageous placing in the signs rather than the houses. One form is still in universal use, and it is exceptionally valuable. By it, each planet has a special association with the signs as a "ruler" or "lord" of one or two among them, and this relation can be best shown in tabular form.

THE RULERSHIPS OF THE SIGNS

	Sun	Leo	Cancer	Moon
	Mercury	Virgo	Gemini	Mercury
	Venus	Libra	Taurus	Venus
Pluto,	Mars	Scorpio	Aries	Mars
	Jupiter	Sagittarius	Pisces	Jupiter or Neptune
	Saturn	Capricorn	Aquarius	Saturn or Uranus

This scheme is easy to learn if it is observed that the signs are arranged in pairs and that the older planets, or those known before the discovery of Uranus, Neptune and Pluto, are rulers of the signs as paired in this way, the sun and moon ruling a pair together. The order of the planets in this rulership is the same as their position in the heavens, again with the sun and moon as an exception.

The two rulerships given to three of the twelve signs in the table is the result of a difference of opinion among present-day astrologers. Some hold to the ancient or "Chaldean" rulerships. Some put the new planets in the places shown. Some seek to avoid trouble by considering the new planets "co-rulers" at the three points of dispute.

A planet has weight when it is in the house it rules. More important, however, than any consideration of these older "dignities," is the fact that a planet also has lordship over any other planets lying in a sign of which it is ruler. Sometimes it will happen that one of them will ultimately rule all the others, directly or indirectly, and this is known as "singleton in disposition." Of all the dignities, this complete disposition is by far the most powerful. It is, however, the least immediately obvious of the focal determinators described in this text.

A "singleton in disposition" will be found in the chart of Gandhi, holding to the older rulerships of the signs. First it is necessary to find a case where one planet, and one only, is in a sign it rules, and in this instance it is Mars in Scorpio. Next it must be seen that all the other planets end up under the rulership of this one, or the Mars here. Scorpio contains not only Mars, but also Mercury and Venus. Aries, which is also ruled by Mars, contains Neptune. This means that Mars directly rules or disposes of three planets, or four out of the ten including itself. Mercury, ruled by Mars, is the lord of Gemini and Virgo, but neither of these signs contain any planets, and so Mercury adds none to the string of those ruled by Mars. This is also true of Neptune, which in the older scheme of rulership is not the lord of any sign. Venus, however, rules Taurus, which contains Pluto and Jupiter, and Libra, which contains the sun, so that Venus adds three to the original four under the Mars disposition, or brings the string up to seven out of ten. Pluto is lord of no sign and makes no contribution, but the sun is lord of Leo, the sign which contains the moon, and Jupiter is the lord of Sagittarius and Pisces, the first of which signs contains Saturn. Thus two more planets, the moon through sun and Venus, and Saturn through Jupiter and Venus, are added to the string under the final rulership of Mars, or nine out of the total ten. Saturn is the lord of Capricorn and Aquarius, but these signs contain no planets, and so Saturn makes no contribution to the string. The moon is lord of Cancer, however, and Cancer contains Uranus, the last of the ten planets, which is thus brought under the rule of Mars through the moon, sun and Venus in order. Mars is thus the undisputed ruler of the chart. This indicates that Gandhi's life is entirely and wholly a task of initiative, or of creative beginnings in every respect.

Summary

In summary of the over-all perspective, the beginner has seen that he takes the various focal determinators in the order by which it is easy to see them in a chart, until he finds the basis for a complete or guiding perspective on the life as a whole. At the same time he also observes the ascendant and sun signs, to see if the horoscope reasonably corresponds to the native's general character and appearance; a rough preliminary check against the possibility of a wrong chart.

In special detail, the beginner has been shown the possibilities in comparing all new horoscopes with the ones he already knows. He has seen the possibilities of over-all understanding when the planets are preponderantly in one kind of house or sign. He has given some attention to the significance of elevated and rising planets, as well as to the strength of planets as the rulers of particular signs.

Detailed Interpretation

He is now ready for detailed interpretation. Here the consideration passes from the differences by which people are distinguished among each other to the everyday activities by which all men carry on their normal lives. The best technique in a complete horoscope interpretation is a careful analysis of each planet in order, although exactly the same result may be obtained by taking each house in turn. If the planets are taken for "delineation," the houses appear as the domains which they rule. If the houses are taken, the planets appear as their lords or administrators. The advantage of working with the planets is that it gives a more dynamic, and usually more interesting, interpretation of the chart.

The first step is to relate each planet to the focal determination of the given horoscope. The second step is to show how its activity is shaped by the house it is in; revealing its activity in connection with everyday affairs. The third step is to indicate the significance of the planet's sign, showing how its activity affects the native's organism or relates the various parts of his life to the whole pattern of the chart. The fourth step is to reveal the planet's common activity with the other planets, as this is established by the aspects between them and shows the direction of emphasis in the life activities. The fifth and last step is to point out the special way in which the planet relates its house and sign position to the chart as a whole.

All these steps except the last have been amply illustrated in connection with interesting or important personages.

A planet is the lord of the sign or signs it rules, according to the table given, and in consequence it becomes the ruler of the house or houses whose cusps fall in the sign or signs in question. If a planet is in a house it rules, it is always able to advance the affairs of that house without interference. Thus Mars in Gandhi's chart rules the first house, and he has no difficulty in carrying out his own enterprises, once he determines what to do. Goethe's Jupiter rules the fourth house, where it is placed; particularly aiding his final creative work on *Faust*, done practically at death's door, and enabling him to put his whole soul into it. Lord Byron's Saturn is in his ninth, ruling it, and his moon is in his second, as ruler also, so that he was preeminently free to express himself in the depths of mentality and also in a broad emotional exploitation of money and resources. Annie Besant's moon in her fourth, as lord of that house, is responsible for her great ultimate emotional capacity, and her Venus in the seventh as ruler enabled her to capitalize handsomely on every opportunity that came her way. Elbert Hubbard's Jupiter in his sixth, as lord of the house, and his Mercury in the ninth as ruler, endow him with an expansive genius both in serving others or getting work out of them on the one hand, and in maneuvering his thinking around to serve his own purposes at all times on the other. Emerson's ruler of his ninth, present in that house, links him with Byron and Elbert Hubbard in a fluid control of his own thinking processes; and the fact that the lord of his eighth is in that house is an indication of the great regenerative power of his philosophy.

When the lord of a house is in another house, the affairs of the one house are made contributory to the other, and this is an important feature of any detailed delineation. Thus Elbert Hubbard's personality (the first house) is really focused in his mind (the ninth) because Venus, ruler of Libra on the first house cusp, is in the ninth, and it has already been seen that he was too often lost in the theoretical considerations of life for his own ultimate good.

One final word is very important at this concluding point in an initial "looking at a horoscope." The theory behind all chart interpretations is that if the pattern of the life's function is known, or accurately charted in experience, it is always possible to find a way for improving the native's circumstances, or leading him into some finer and happier situation. The real purpose in a study of astrology should be not the satisfaction of an intellectual curiosity, but ultimately the desire to be equipped, if only in a layman's fashion, for helping others to solve their problems. The basis of such an equipment, sketched all too briefly here because of the harsh but very real limitations of space, has comprised these seven chapters, and pointed to the way in which it can be done. In brief, this is how to look at a horoscope.

ADDENDA

In addition to the ten planets, the three following symbols are very commonly found in charts. They are of minor importance, relatively speaking, and for that reason are not introduced in this elementary text. However, it is better for the beginner to know what they are, and what they mean in a very general way, than to be puzzled by them when he encounters them.

☊ Dragon's head, a point of general "protection" in the chart.

☋ Dragon's tail, a point of "self-undoing."

⊕ Part of Fortune, a point where self-interest is particularly emphasized.

HOW TO MAKE
A HOROSCOPE

PUTTING UP THE WHEEL

FEW THINGS are as fascinating as putting up a horoscope, and watching its patterns unfold on a sheet of paper. Beginners in astrology however will often go out of their way to make the task harder than necessary. Thus they jump to the conclusion that horoscopic calculation involves a lot of difficult mathematics. They fail to realize that all the complicated computations have been performed for them in advance, and are incorporated in quite simple tables readily available and easy to use. They assume that it is quite out of the question for an average person to understand what the mathematical side of astrology is all about. They make sheer drudgery out of the procedures, either by trying to commit them to memory in a thoroughly blind fashion, or by following the uninformative directions of a printed form no less blindly.

The Two Operations

Making a horoscope has two parts. First is finding the position of the horoscopic wheel in the heavens. This is the matter of locating the houses and signs. Second is determining the location of the planets, or putting them in place by house and sign. These two operations are entirely separate procedures.

The position of the horoscopic wheel for a daily time and place, commonly at either midnight or noon at the Greenwich or prime meridian passing through the 1675 observatory in a southeast borough of London in England, is given in the astrological ephemerides currently in print for more than a century back. If birth did not occur in the London area or elsewhere at 0° geographical longitude, a simple correction is made to adjust to that circumstance. This of course is in order to make use of the ephemeris consulted.

If birth did not occur at the zero hour or midnight beginning the day, if the one form of ephemeris is used, or at noon if the other, a similar and equally simple correction is made to adjust for this second contingency. These steps are in order to locate the horizon of a living individuality properly and accurately in the heavenly scheme of things. To be noted parenthetically is that the midnight-based ephemeris is a recent innovation, and in consequence is not encountered except for relatively recent years.

With these preliminary corrections made to the extent they are necessary, the elements of the horoscopic wheel can be taken from the two kinds of tables where the more intricate mathematical calculations have already been performed for the astrologer. With the aid primarily of one of the convenient sets of tabulations, the horoscope can be half completed quickly and quite handily. With the notation, in the familiar circular diagram, of the data obtained from the other set of tables the horoscope is complete and ready for interpretation.

The Two Kinds of Tables

The astrological ephemeris is needed for both operations in the calculation of a horoscope. These ephemerides are usually published annually, but sometimes for a series of years. No element of any year is ever precisely duplicated in any other, however, and so there is no practical substitution among them even if leap

years are matched. Each monthly tabulation of planetary factors also includes a column of sidereal time,
which will be explained shortly, and this special column identifies the heavenly position of any horoscopic
wheel for a birth on the prime meridian at the midnight or noon of the particular ephemeris consulted.
Here in consequence is the basis of the initial operation in putting up the horoscopic chart. In its other
details the ephemeris is the source of the information
needed for determining the positions of the planets at
birth.

The other kind of tables are published separately,
since they do not change from year to year and only
rather imperceptibly from century to century. They are
known as Tables of Houses, and they give the zodiacal positions of the twelve houses of the horoscope
once its own or individual prime meridian has been
established. Preparation must now be made for the
consideration of the fundamental wheel-diagram in detail, and of its celestial placement in any specific instance.

The Wheel-Diagram

A beginner must be familiar, at the outset, with the
form of a horoscope. The four example charts as well
as the illustrative ones in the preceding chapters are
presented in what has become the almost universal
custom in preparation. Individual astrologers will have
their characteristic differences of indication or notation, but seldom of any extreme nature. In the present
or 1969 revision of this part of the book concerned
with the making of the horoscope, and in all the larger
volumes of the Sabian series, a minor economy of identification of planetary place by sign still found in the
earlier pages of this text and also in the *Guide to Horo-*

scope Interpretation has been abandoned as an idiosyncrasy of the author. The omission of the zodiacal symbol in connection with each planet, which was his habit in his own early practice, came to prove more confusing than helpful.

In its diagram form the horoscope consists of a circle with a horizontal and perpendicular division into quarters, and with each quarter further divided into three equal wedge-shaped sections to make twelve in all. The dividing lines are not brought to center but only to a central circle that sometimes is considered to represent the earth, but that primarily serves to spare the eye from a measure of visual distraction. These twelve segments shown by actual line printed or drawn are the identification of the houses of the chart.

The signs are divided in their circle in exactly the same way as the houses, but they are not shown directly in the horoscopic wheel. Instead of putting in the lines of another twelve pielike divisions, with results that can be very confusing to the eye even when different colors are used, the degrees or perhaps degrees and minutes of the zodiacal sign corresponding to the cusp or beginning of each house together with the symbol for the sign are noted at the line indicating the house. Except in the case of the ascendant or first house the minutes are generally omitted and the zodiacal point rounded to the next full degree, and not infrequently this is the procedure at the ascendant. In similar fashion the zodiacal sign, degrees and minutes of position of a planet are written in the usual order of reading next to the planetary symbol which in its turn is placed in the diagram in closest possible juxtaposition to the house lines on the one side or the other. In other words, except most rarely, there is no attempt by the astrologer to give the eye any indication of the actual spacing of these bodies in house and sign but instead the emphasis is on the house cusps in order to facilitate delineation.

What is most important to realize at this point is that the planets in an astrological chart are thus indicated in their heavenly positions of two altogether different sorts, but both at the same time. Their place by house is seen directly, and their location by sign is indicated indirectly through the notation of zodiacal degrees and minutes. Their dual signification can in this manner be seen as the fundamental basis of all individuality in a personal horoscope.

The Elementary Background

If the beginner is starting with making the horoscope rather than looking at the horoscope, he will have to learn the numbers of the houses and the symbols of both the signs and the planets at this point. He will have to know that a sign of the zodiac consists of thirty degrees, and any degree of sixty minutes of which each minute comprises sixty seconds. He must recognize the symbol of a degree (°), a minute of a degree ('), a second of a degree ("), an hour (h), a minute of an hour (m), and a second of an hour (s). The numbering of the houses may well be shown as a whole at this point, but it already has been seen in the four diagrams beginning on page 15. The scheme of the signs may also be presented as a whole at this point, but the symbols for each of them have been introduced beginning on page 60. Their arrangement in pairs of opposites, necessary to know by heart in any use of a Tables of Houses, has been tabulated on page 82. An introduction and explanation of the symbols for the planets begins on page 30.

THE SCHEMATIC BASIS OF HOUSES AND SIGNS

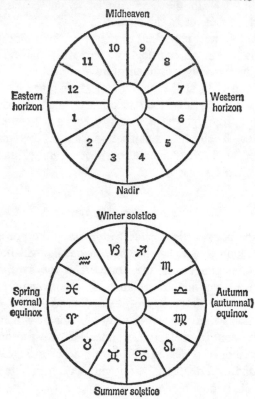

The young student must be particularly careful not to confuse geographic or terrestrial with astronomic or celestial longitude, or in an alternative way of saying it he must keep a complete line of separation between what is his concern on a map or in connection with the surface of the earth on the one hand and what requires his attention in the heavens when dealing with the zodiac on the other. By the same token he must remember the same distinction between the two kinds of latitude even if only one of them enters the picture in all usual or more familiar horoscopic procedures. In the meanwhile he must be patient, since there will not be too many things or any at all of appreciable complication for him to have in mind in order to function effectively at almost the very start.

How the Horoscope Operates

Much of the supposed difficulty in astrology will disappear if the beginner will take a spare quarter-hour, and use it to get an effective grasp of the horoscope's manner of operation. What lies before him on a sheet of paper is a chart of the planetary bodies that in its nature is much like a photograph of their arrangement in the heavens. This can be made clear for him by diagram, but it is necessary that he prepare himself for a little shock when he sees just where north, east and the like are placed in the astrological symbolism. However, he will not get very far if he starts in to quarrel with things because they are different. If he wanted to study French he would adapt himself sooner or later to the French way of thinking about things, and he must realize that the practitioners of astrology have their own ways of procedure as just about everybody else has. They may seem unnecessarily individualistic at times, but they have the tradition of many centuries behind them.

The person who looks at a horoscope is sitting to all intents and purposes at an immense distance out in space on an extension of the north pole. The twelve horoscopic houses that he sees are formed in the equator of the earth, but it is an equator also extended like the north pole out into the whole heavens until it becomes a gigantic saucer or hoop. The houses thus can be visualized as a heavenly wheel of which the earth's two poles would be the axle. The beginner can imagine the great hoop to be filled in with thin white paper, in the manner of the one through which animals jump in a circus, or he can think of it as an immensely round photographic plate on which an exposure is made by the planets at the moment of birth. Irrespective of how near the surface of the paper or plate the planets and all the true and distant stars may be or how far away, whether on the observer's side or the other, they are seen from such an infinite distance that their relations with each other are all flattened out and brought together in the patterns of the one horoscopic wheel and the celestial vault of which it is a part.

Thus the heavenly bodies are placed where they actually are seen to lie in the great wheel. The question of the astrological house in which each will be found depends on the relation of that illimitable saucer in the skies, or what technically is the celestial equator,

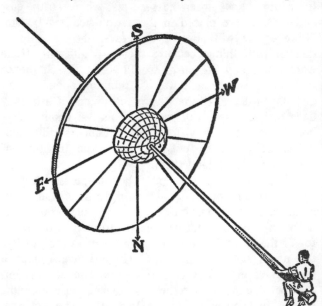

with the particular locality of birth on the surface of the earth. Emergence into existence as a living human entity establishes a horizon that represents the given particularity of each and every individual, and this becomes the factor of fundamental significance in the horoscopic analysis. The left-hand point or east in a horoscope, and the right-hand point or west, together identify or show the horizon that is created very literally and physically at the time and place of birth. The upper point or south, and the lower point or north, together locate or show the individual prime meridian that passes directly overhead each native at the moment he is born.

The Compass Directions in Astrology

The beginner will be very wise at this point to put the book down for a few minutes, and to step out into some convenient open space. If he extends both arms wide, and turns around very slowly, he will describe the horizon actually found in any horoscope made for the moment and place of this act on his part. The ascendant is where the sun actually would rise, and the descendant where it would set. Then, if he will look directly over his head he will see a point in the skies that will lie on the same meridian where at true noon the sun would be found. Probably at that sundial noon the sun will lie to the south of him, although it will be to his north if he himself is far enough to the south in geographic latitude for the particular time of year. This meridian passing overhead at any significant moment in his affairs as well as at birth, and passing through the sun at true noon, is the midheaven or south point in astrological language. It is called south for the simple but not altogether logical reason that the planets when placed here in the horoscopic diagramming are seen to the south by most of the people

in the world. The point directly underfoot and beyond
the earth on the other side is on the same great circle
of this personal prime meridian, and in astrological
language it is the nadir or north point that is not literally or precisely the same as the astronomical nadir
in a particular opposition with the zenith. Nadir as a
word is merely given an additional and horoscopic
meaning.

Thus east, west, south and north are terms of special
astrological significance. The horizon points east and
west are in literally correct conformity with everyday
usage, but the south and north designations at the meridian are only directions of the compass in a very
special sense. Most importantly for the beginner however, it must be noted that these directions exactly
reverse those universally employed in geographic maps.
The original idea in this was probably to remind the
interpreter of the horoscope that he was looking up
at the sky, so to speak, and not down onto the surface
of the earth.

The Use of Time to Show Circle Position

For reasons that probably seemed valid to the astrologers of early generations in their art, position on
this circle of the houses was called time. Actually it is
nothing of the sort in any usual sense, but is merely a
case of dividing the circle into twenty-four hours instead of 360 degrees. More specifically this measure is
known as sidereal time, and often identified as just S.T.
While it is identical with the astronomer's sidereal time,
it has nothing to do with any sort of clock measure. A
definite conception of the proposition at this point may
save considerable confusion in later mathematical operations.

To make a horoscope it is necessary first of all to take
an ephemeris for the year of birth, and first find the

S.T. or sidereal time for the day of the event. This is sometimes provided for midnight, but always for noon in the tables for earlier years. It is rather universally given for Greenwich, although one recent and short-lived ephemeris was calculated for Philadelphia. It identifies the point on the celestial equator, or the great heavenly hoop represented by the sheet of paper on which a horoscope is diagrammed, that is crossed by the meridian overhead either at midnight or noon and in the usual case at Greenwich. This S.T. is put down as the starting point in calculation. It however should always be taken for the midnight or noon immediately preceding birth, and this can be a day before as will be illustrated shortly. The reason for going back in such a fashion is to encourage accuracy by following an accustomed procedure in every computation in horoscopy. It is a studied policy of performing all mathematical operations by addition rather than subtraction if reasonably possible. A factor strikingly peculiar to astrology is that the mind whether of a young student or an experienced practitioner is likely to get ahead of itself in fascination with what is unfolding as the chart is prepared, and consequently is apt to have an embarrassing stutter in the dull chore of figuring and thus even slip into an unrealized error in delineation.

The Proper Time of Birth

What is next needed in making a horoscope is the proper time of birth. Obtaining this may be the greatest problem the beginner will face. There are means for compensating the rather common deficiencies of information concerning the reasonably precise hour and minute of the arrival of the newborn citizen into his world of trial and error, but accuracy in the employment of these corrective procedures requires high skill and long experience and hence any more than this casual reference to them has no place in an introductory manual. A novice however cannot start too early in a close questioning or persistent checking of the sources of the data on which he must lean. He can suggest ways of refreshing memory, or he can draw out relationships to other events or contributing circumstances. When it comes to the place of birth he may have to consult an atlas to get the correct geographic longitude and latitude he will require from the start in his calculations.

It may seem that there is altogether too much promise of complication or confusion of factors for the average neophyte to face in putting up a horoscope, but the problems he will meet are all minor ones. One of the most serious possibilities would be a lack of alertness to the chance of mistake at the very start of calculation. Thus all horoscopes are calculated from the local mean time, which is often abbreviated as L.M.T. This is the mean time at the exact geographic longitude of birth, and it nearly always requires a correction from the standard time shown almost universally by the world's clocks. While there are almost continual adjustments in astrological mathematics, they are simple enough and for the major part quite necessary. Meeting these necessities in smooth routine can become a species of fun in performance, or can defeat the monotony of any series of procedures followed blindly by rigid rule.

New York City, at this point a convenient example of adjustments to be made, is situated at 74° west geographic longitude but it uses eastern standard time which is based on a time meridian established at 75° west. If its clocks show 3:27 p.m., the astrological time or L.M.T. is 3:31 p.m. This correction is at the rate of four minutes for each degree of geographic longitude, or a fifteenth of the hour marked off at each time meridian or as from 60° to 75° in this instance. Correcting is by addition if toward the east or back in the direction of the prime meridian at Greenwich, but by subtraction if toward the west as with Annapolis at 76°30′ west where the difference of a degree and a half would mean an adjustment by six minutes and a L.M.T. of 3:21 p.m. compared with New York City's L.M.T. of 3:31 p.m. The beginner can avoid an easy stutter of mind here by remembering that where the sun gets first, it's later.

Various Kinds of Time

It is important to realize that the designation of ordinary time as mean does not identify any sort of difference with which the astrologer ever needs to be concerned, since mean time is the only basic durational measure he might ever be likely to encounter. All clocks around the globe show it, either directly or as standardized in geographic zones or advanced by an hour in summer or war time or other emergency. What the designation indicates is the time created by an averaged rather than an actual sun. This of course is a way of speaking, since it hardly is necessary to point out that it really is the earth and not the sun that is doing the moving in the celestial mechanics. The real or precise crossing of the midheaven meridian by the sun to mark off a true noon each day is irregular in a small way that has no possible astrological significance. In February the sun does not reach the midheaven until fifteen minutes of mean time after noon, and in November it is there ahead of itself in the same interval of mean measure. Its actually irregular movement is designated as apparent, or apparent solar or sundial time.

Standard time can be a genuine annoyance to astrologers, since geographic sections may not be at all consistent in determining the zone in which they will function. An extreme case of this provided by the decision of Great Britain, at the time these pages are under revision, to adopt Central European Time for its standard although actually situated on the prime meridian. Daylight saving or summer or war time can constitute an even greater annoyance because of irregularity in the dates of its effectiveness and possibly also because of some uncertainty of the area in which it is effective.

Why Corrections Are Necessary

With the local mean time of birth obtained, the beginner is ready to proceed. He makes his start by putting down the S.T. of the midnight or noon preceding the moment of birth, and now as he finds them necessary he must make the two corrections to which his attention already has been called. This of course is over and above the adjustments he may have made in determining the L.M.T. and he may have a very fascinating insight into the underlying unity of the great world about him, once he is able to observe the perfection with which everything with all the eccentricities yet dovetails into everything else through the universal mathematics of experience. Thus he may find it very profitable, as an aid to understanding, to take any convenient ephemeris at this stage of things and examine the column of sidereal time for any month at random and notice the regularity of its change from day to day. He should check this for a week or so in the tabulations in order to have a mental picture of the rhythm, and then ask himself what the progression in these hours and minutes represents in general or quite apart from astrology and the horoscope. Most simply it is nothing more than the movement of the sun, or the differences in the heavens that add up the midnights or noons as the case may be and thereupon measure the sun's yearly pilgrimage through the sky. It is a very regular procedure, practically the same year after year. Its principal variation results from the recurrences of the extra leap-year day.

The S.T. of the individual horoscope always indicates the point on the house circle that in essence is directly overhead, or through which more correctly the overhead meridian will pass at a given time and place. If the birth does not occur on the earth's prime meridian or at 0° of geographic longitude, but rather at some location to the west on the surface of the earth, the heavens obviously must keep on turning to get the S.T. for the given horoscope on the actual overhead meridian. While this is going on the sun necessarily continues with the daily quota of its annual movement. This is very slight on the whole, yet it definitely changes the S.T. point in that day-by-day rhythm the beginner has noted in the ephemeris. In other words, while the whole heavens turn to reach the day's S.T. for a given birthplace, that S.T. itself is also advancing on its own account in these same heavens. A correction normally must be added to adjust for this.

What has to be done to find the correction is to divide this particular movement of the S.T. for the whole day into parts that will correspond to the geographic sections of the globe over which the sun will pass in the course of the day, or more specifically up to the place of birth. By making this division it is found that 9.86 seconds of sidereal time or ten seconds in round figures will equate with fifteen degrees of geographic longitude. Hence 9.86s or a rounded 10s will have exact correspondence to a usual standard time zone. As illustration, New York City is slightly less than five hours of time difference west from Greenwich and the correction is slightly less than 50s rounded or is 49s precisely for the first of the example charts. This T.D. or time-difference relation to Greenwich must be noted preliminarily in the case of every horoscope.

If the S.T. of an individual horoscope is for a birthplace lying east of the earth's prime meridian, as in the case of the third of the example charts or the one calculated for Moscow, the correction must be subtracted. This obviously is necessary because if the sun gets there first in comparison with points on the earth's prime meridian or westward from it, the S.T. of the sun's daily movement is not as far along as at the midnight or noon of the ephemeris. Thus a time difference from Greenwich of 2h 30m to the east calls for a subtracted correction of 25s both in round figures and precisely. Conformity here to the policy of always adding in the astrological procedures would of course be needlessly cumbersome. This adjustment of 9.86s precisely or 10s in round terms is known as the correction of mean to sidereal time, and a tabulation for the use of it precisely is provided on the next page. However, while it may be wise for the professional astrologer to make this correction in the more exact terms and for the beginner to get in the habit of doing so, there is seldom an instance where the difference has any practical significance. Furthermore, in the actual practice of horoscopy, the curtailment of available hours or even minutes to be used for the basic calculations means that a great deal of rounding of figures must be employed.

A Beginner's Dilemma

The newcomer to astrology now encounters what is quite a dilemma at times. He may feel himself in the impasse of the five-year-old youngster who, in the baffling process of adjustment to adult ways, has approbation for a bit of mischief because company at the house finds it amusingly cute and then a few days later receives a severe scolding for the same conduct because it is misbehavior. If at the start the neophyte is encouraged to make these corrections involving not only minutes but seconds of the minutes with the help of the table for precise correction of mean or clock to astro-

CORRECTION, MEAN TO SIDEREAL TIME

Mean time	Add	Mean time	Add	Mean time	Add	Mean time	Add
1h 0m	9.86s	1m	0.16s	25m	4.11s	49m	8.05s
2 0	19.71	2	0.33	26	4.27	50	8.21
3 0	29.57	3	0.49	27	4.43	51	8.38
4 0	39.43	4	0.66	28	4.60	52	8.54
5 0	49.28	5	0.82	29	4.76	53	8.71
6 0	59.14	6	0.99	30	4.93	54	8.87
7 1	9.00	7	1.15	31	5.09	55	9.03
8 1	18.85	8	1.31	32	5.26	56	9.20
9 1	28.71	9	1.48	33	5.42	57	9.36
10 1	38.57	10	1.64	34	5.58	58	9.53
11 1	48.42	11	1.81	35	5.75	59	9.69
12 1	58.28	12	1.97	36	5.91	60	9.86
13 2	8.13	13	2.14	37	6.08		
14 2	17.99	14	2.30	38	6.24		
15 2	27.85	15	2.46	39	6.41		
16 2	37.70	16	2.63	40	6.57		
17 2	47.56	17	2.79	41	.6.73		
18 2	57.42	18	2.96	42	6.90		
19 3	7.27	19	3.12	43	7.06		
20 3	17.13	20	3.28	44	7.23		
21 3	26.99	21	3.45	45	7.39		
22 3	36.84	22	3.61	46	7.56		
23 3	46.70	23	3.78	47	7.72		
24 3	56.56	24	3.94	48	7.88		

logical or sidereal time, and then is told in usual practice he may round 9.86s to 10s and actually might be told further that in many cases he could use a near fifteen-degree meridian for the place adjustment, he may wonder what is what.

"When am I to be exact, and when is it unnecessary to be so?" he might well ask. "How inexact can I be when it is all right to be inexact?"

There is a great deal of difference between a lack of precision, and a capacity for establishing a proper plateau of preciseness. Thus in modern technology a mechanical refinement to a hundredth of an inch may be more than adequate in some instances whereas in others the exactness necessary may be to a thousandth of an inch. In astrology the seconds of arc or time are frequently eliminated from consideration by ignoring them or rounding them to minutes, whether of sidereal time or in the zodiac, and the minutes in turn are rather commonly disregarded in a rounding to parts or wholes of hours or degrees. This may seem to be imprecision, but as done intelligently it is a commonplace of all skilled computation. The extent to which it is proper is whether or not in a given operation the difference involved is significant. Suggestions concerning the procedure are incorporated in these pages as they may be pertinent in an introductory text, and the niceties of astrological mathematics as the background of the expert's skill have a broader consideration in the author's *Scope of Astrological Prediction.*

For the sake of the beginner's ultimate excellence in horoscopic analysis he should be as precise as possible in his arithmetic procedures, even if no more than as practice in a refinement of his skills. This can help him build to the capacity for delineation of a nativity, such as can come to its full only by gradual steps in sound experience. In any case the charts he retains for his own record or private information should have

complete notation of his procedures, so that in later
reference to them by himself or others it can be seen
to what extent he has averaged out the minutiae of
differences he has considered insignificant.

To be especially noted is that throughout the text-
books, of which this is the introductory manual, there
is one special modification of the mathematician's manner of rounding numbers or say taking 4°29′ as 4° and
4°30′ as 5°. Thus in the case of zodiacal degrees, but
only in that case, a next full degree is always taken
even if the previous one actually has a most minuscule
increment. Thus 15°0′1″ is rounded to 16° for the sake
of possible recourse to the symbolization of the zodiacal degrees that have their full exposition in the
author's *Sabian Symbols in Astrology*.

The Adjustment for Time of Birth

The other of the two operations in locating the
wheel-diagram is to correct the time of birth from
mean to sidereal if the event has not occurred at the
precise Greenwich midnight or noon of the ephemeris
from which the S.T. of the midnight or noon is taken.
Behind this second correction in putting up the horoscope is the same proposition as in adjusting the S.T.
of the midheaven for the geographical place of birth.
It has been seen if not quite in these terms that twenty-
four hours of clock time correspond to twenty-four
hours, three minutes and fifty-six-odd seconds of true
circle measurement as in sidereal time. Since a clock
hour is shorter in this connection each one of them,
when it comes to determining position on the house
circle or in a sense indicating a space factor, must be
lengthened by the precise 9.86s or rounded 10s that
has been the correction in the first operation. The whole
procedure will be illustrated in the cases of the four
example charts. In other words there first will be

the location of the whole wheel in the heavens, and then there will be the necessary notation of all twelve house cusps in their zodiacal correspondence to complete the horoscope.

The Function of Geographic Latitude

With the S.T. of the midheaven of the individual horoscope determined by adding to the corrected S.T. of the place of birth the corrected interval of time from the previous midnight or noon to the moment of birth, the location of all twelve house cusps in the zodiacal equivalents needed for the placement of the planetary elements in the wheel-diagram can be copied out of the Tables of Houses. At this point the terrestrial horizon comes into consideration. The beginner has been asked to stand out in the open with arms outstretched horizontally and to turn clear around to describe his horizon of that place and moment to himself in his visualization of a horoscope's functioning. What is represented is in all respects the basic plane or ground of his personal existence, and its particular position in the heavenly scheme of astrology is determined by the geographic latitude of the birthplace. The cusps needed in their zodiacal correspondence are found in the Tables of Houses at the proper latitude. As already noted, the minor ones usually together with the midheaven and nadir are rounded to the even next degree and the ascendant and descendant are by contrast brought generally to degrees and minutes of preciseness or perhaps rounded to quarters or tenths of a degree. At the time of first writing and now of the revision of this text there are two published tabulations of house cusps adequate for the standards of workmanship recommended in the Sabian exposition and needed in all widely accepted horoscopy. The calculations by Joseph G. Dalton were made available in 1893 in his *Spherical*

Basis of Astrology and those by Hugh S. Rice were issued in 1944 as the *American Astrology Tables of Houses.*

Summary

In summary, what has the beginner learned in Section One of how to make rather than how to look at a horoscope? He has been introduced to all the basic elements of horoscopic mathematics, and has been shown how to proceed in accomplishing the first of the two tasks in establishing an individual horoscopic wheel in the heavens. He has been brought face-to-face with the distinction between troublemaking carelessness and intelligent fluidity, and shown the value of schooled or consistent method in all astrological procedure. He has been assured that all computations of unusual complexity, or beyond the average skills of everyday life, have been performed for him in advance and with the results readily available in printed form. He has been introduced to the two kinds of tabulations he must employ continually, or the ephemeris and the Tables of Houses, and prepared for using them effectively and without appreciable difficulty. He has been given a detailed visualization and explanation of the nature of the horoscopic map or wheel-diagram he must learn to make for himself, so that he can know exactly what he is doing and thus be less likely to let some error slip by him. He has been drilled in the nature of apparent, mean, standard, daylight saving and war time on the one hand and the species of circle measurement known as sidereal time on the other. He has been helped to understand the relations among these different sorts of time, and what necessity for correction arises in considering them in their connection with each other.

The Example Horoscopes

The example charts are presented at this point in the bare skeleton of their structure, to the end that the beginner may concentrate on the establishment in the heavens in necessary zodiacal correspondences of the twelve horoscopic houses created at the birthplace at the time of birth. The completed wheel-diagrams are presented later, beginning on page 157.

Example I is prepared from a noon ephemeris and Dalton's Tables of Houses. The birth data is July 4, 1969, New York City, 3:06 p.m., L.M.T. The calculation is as follows:

S.T. Greenwich noon, July 4th:	6h	49m	17s
Correction for 73°57′ west longitude:			49
Elapsed time, noon to birth:	3	6	
Its correction to sidereal time:			31
	9	56	37

The T.D. or time difference from Greenwich of 4h 56m requires a first correction by the table of 48.63s, which rounds to the 49s used. With its closeness to the 75° meridian, that T.D. of 5h at the approximate 10s per hour would give a correction of 50s as a more than adequate approximation for the calculation. By the same token, in the case of the second correction, the precise 30.56s rounded to 31s is not significantly different from the 30s derived from taking an even 3h at 10s per hour. In Dalton's tabulations a S.T. of 9h 56m 52s is only a hairsbreadth more than the 9h 56m 37s found to be the S.T. of the horoscope's midheaven, and in consequence Leo 27° is taken for this example with virtually no rounding involved.

Example II is prepared from a midnight ephemeris and Dalton's Tables of Houses. The birth data is De-

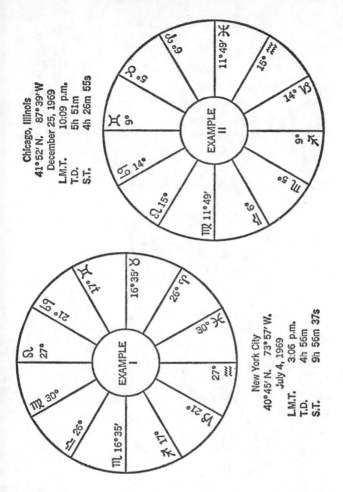

Chicago, Illinois
41°52'N. 87°39'W
December 25, 1969
L.M.T. 10:09 p.m.
T.D. 5h 51m
S.T. 4h 26m 55s

EXAMPLE II

♓ 11°49'
♒ 15°
♑ 14°
♐ 9°
♏ 5°
♎ 6°
♍ 11°49'
♌ 15°
♋ 14°
♊ 9°
♉ 5°
♈ 6°

New York City
40°45'N. 73°57'W.
July 4, 1969
L.M.T. 3:06 p.m.
T.D. 4h 56m
S.T. 9h 56m 37s

EXAMPLE I

♈ 17°
♉ 16°35'
♊ 21°
♋ 26°
♌ 27°
♍ 30°
♎ 26°
♏ 16°35'
♐ 17°
♑ 21°
♒ 27°
♓ 30°

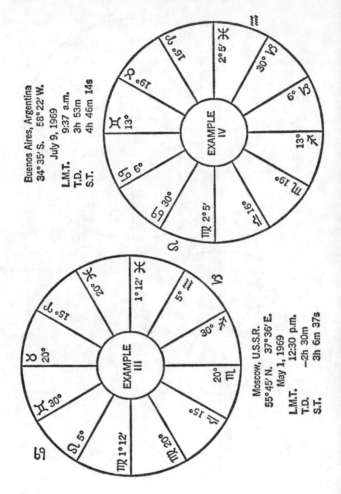

Moscow, U.S.S.R.
55°45'N.　37°36'E.
May 1, 1969
L.M.T.　12:30 p.m.
T.D.　−2h 30m
S.T.　3h 6m 37s

EXAMPLE
III

Buenos Aires, Argentina
34°35'S.　58°22'W.
July 9, 1969
9:37 a.m.
L.M.T.
T.D.　3h 53m
S.T.　4h 46m 14s

EXAMPLE
IV

cember 25, 1969, Chicago, 10:09 p.m., L.M.T. The
calculation is as follows:

S.T. Greenwich midnight, December 25th:	6h	13m	19s
Correction for 87°39' west longitude:			58
Elapsed time, midnight to birth:	22	9	
Its correction to sidereal time:		3	38
	28	26	55
(−)	24		
	4	26	55

As is done here, 24h or 360° may always be added or
subtracted in the course of calculation in hours or degrees around a circle. The T.D. of 5h 51m requires a
first correction of 57.66s, which rounds to the 58s used.
To work from a time meridian nearby or in this case
by about two and a half degrees of terrestrial longitude, in a procedure that is quite legitimate in approximate computation, would mean taking the T.D. as 6h
and to correct at 10s per hour or by what in this instance would be an adjustment of 60s or 1m. The difference in S.T. of 2s could only have significance most
extraordinarily. With the second correction of a precise
3m 38.32s rounded to 3m 38s in usual mathematical
practice, in comparison with an approximate 3m 40s
for an even 22h, is this close in the approximation
because 9m of elapsed time from midnight are ignored.
To take them into account would add 1s more and
make the approximate correction 3m 41s. Even then
the 3s of difference could hardly be of any importance,
but a failure to make any correction could put a different zodiacal degree on some or all of the house
cusps of the horoscope. In this example the midheaven
then would move back to Gemini 8° and the whole
more subtle import of the wheel would be altered. In
the Dalton tables the S.T. for an even Gemini 8° midheaven is 4h 24m 25s, and for an even Gemini 9° is
4h 29m 11s. The S.T. of 4h 26m 55s for the individual

example horoscope is between these points and therefore the next full or even degree of Gemini 9° is recognized as its proper midheaven.

Parenthetically, if the beginner wishes to be sure
whether he is using a midnight or a noon ephemeris,
he can turn to March and if the S.T. shown there is
changing to 12h 0m 0s its positions are for midnight
and if changing to 0h 0m 0s the planetary places are
for noon and of course for Greenwich in both cases.

Example III is prepared from a noon ephemeris and
Dalton's Tables of Houses. The birth data is May 1,
1969 (N.S.), Moscow, 12:30 p.m., L.M.T. The calculation is as follows:

S.T. Greenwich noon, May 1st:		2h	36m 57s
Correction for 37°36′ east longitude:	(−)		25
		2	36 32
Elapsed time, noon to birth:			30
Its correction to sidereal time:			5
		3	6 37

The abbreviation N.S. is for new style or the Gregorian
calendar now in worldwide use. It was only early
in the present century that Russia and other eastern
countries changed from the older Julian calendar now
designated O.S. for old style. The beginner may never
encounter the confusion that can result from an er-
roneous identification of dates here. It is possible that
people born in the areas in question from March 1,
1800 (O.S.), to March 1, 1900 (O.S.), will have to
add twelve days, or from March 1, 1900 (O.S.) to the
adoption of the new calendar will have to add thirteen
to have their birthdays correct in today's proper (N.S.)
designation.

The T.D. in this example of 2h 30m requires a first
correction of 24.64s, which rounds to the 25s that
would be obtained for two and a half hours at the

approximate 10s per hour. Because of east terrestrial longitude of birth, this is subtracted. The second correction is for a mere half hour, but for the sake of a regular rhythm of routine it should be made as shown. In the Dalton tables the S.T. for an even Taurus 19° on the midheaven is 3h 6m 10s, or very slightly less than the S.T. of the individual midheaven in the case here of 3h 6m 37s, but by the regular procedure adopted in these texts the next full degree or Taurus 20° is taken.

Southern Hemisphere Horoscopes

A horoscope for the southern hemisphere is prepared in precisely the same fashion as one for the northern hemisphere, with a single and simple modification. The tilt of the horizon in places below the terrestrial equator is the reverse of its tilt in the geographic north at the same point in the house circle, and the result is that the apparent distortion of the houses when seen in their zodiacal correspondence in the northern hemisphere will be complemented by the mirror image of this distortion in the southern one. In a way of putting the matter and going back to preliminaries, if more than a quarter of the zodiac appears between the midheaven and ascendant relative to a given quarter of the globe's surface there will be correspondingly less than a quarter left to divide among the other cusps on the same side or between the ascendant and the nadir. This apparent house distortion is what as a constant phenomenon in all horoscopes is reversed between the nadir and midheaven through the descendant. The geographical shift in hemisphere to the other side of the terrestrial equator thereupon additionally reverses the total basic distortion in the zodiacal equivalences because of the change in horizon due to the different curvature of the earth away from its equa-

tor. All that is necessary mathematically is to add 12h
to the S.T. of the individual southern-hemisphere horoscope in order to get the house cusps in their mirror
image zodiacally from the Tables of Houses, but then
to be careful to take the signs opposite at each cusp
from the sign shown in the Tables of Houses when
the 12h are added thus temporarily to the proper
S.T.

Example IV is prepared from a noon ephemeris and
Dalton's Tables of Houses. The birth data is July 9,
1969, Buenos Aires, 9:37 a.m., L.M.T., and this is
the only one of the four examples where calculation is
from a previous midnight or noon and as follows:

S.T. Greenwich noon, July 8th:		7h	5m	3s
Correction for 58°22′ west longitude:				38
Elapsed time, noon to birth:		21	37	
Its correction to sidereal time:			3	33
		28	46	14
	(−) 24			
		4	46	14
To reverse zodiacal distortion	(+) 12			
		16	46	14

The T.D. of 3h 53m by the table requires a first correction of 38.28s rounding to 38s, and a second one
for the elapsed time of 21h 37m is 3m 33.07s rounding
to 3m 33s. To be noted is that the geographic longitude of birth is not too close to the 60° meridian although closer than to 45° west. The 4h of time span
to 60° multiplied by 10s for each would give an approximate correction of 40s, and the difference of 2s would
have little possible significance. Taking the elapsed
time as twenty-two and a half hours would by the approximate 10s per hour give 225s or 3m 45s for a correction that in virtually any possible case would be
adequate but with 12s difference yet beginning to ap-

proach a risk of lack of precision. In the Dalton tables the sidereal time for an even Sagittarius 13° for a horoscopic midheaven is 16h 46m 16s and this is within 2s of exact conformity to the 16h 46m 14s of the fourth example chart's prime meridian. It therefore is taken for this wheel-diagram, but as Gemini 13°.

Determining the Ascendant

In copying the house cusps out of the Tables of Houses the beginner has no problem if birth has taken place at a location found on an even degree of geographic latitude, and at a time that has produced an even degree of some sign on the midheaven when he is using the Dalton tabulations. He already has encountered the adjustment necessary when the individual S.T. of a horoscope lies between the S.T. of one midheaven degree and the next, and in a measure this process must be repeated with the five other cusps he must establish in the wheel-diagram. The cusps of houses four to nine are exactly opposite in zodiacal position to the midheaven and on through the third in order, and are not needed in the tables. If the birthplace does not lie on an even degree of geographic latitude there is a second adjustment, but this usually is slight and easy to approximate.

Since it is the general custom to indicate the ascendant of a horoscope in degrees and minutes, rather than the rounded degrees of other cusps, the beginner in consequence faces the need for at least a relative precision in making what usually is an adjustment in two ways. This is particularly a necessity for all the cusps if there is to be any recourse to the zodiacal degree symbols. The procedure need not be confusing if each adjustment is made in its own turn, and always by addition from a lesser to a greater longitude in the zodiacal positions. In the case of the minor cusps an estimation is sufficient and this usually is adequate if taken to quarters or tenths of degrees, whichever proves to be the easier in facilitation of the rounding. Because the ascendant should be calculated to minutes, the best practice locates it immediately after determining the position of the midheaven and the details of the process can be illustrated in connection with the example horoscopes.

Example I is a case where only a single adjustment is really necessary in locating the ascendant in its zodiacal correspondence. This is because its individual S.T. is only 15s short of the S.T. of a precise Leo 27° midheaven, and such a small difference could hardly ever be a matter of significance for any of the twelve cusps or call for any consideration here. The adjustment for geographic latitude by contrast always tends to be slight, if seldom to this extent, and should be taken into account except in very approximate calculation. The place of birth in this first example is at 40°45′ north latitude or a quarter of the way south from the 41st to the 40th parallel. In Dalton's tabulations, in the column of house cusps established by a Leo 27° midheaven, the first house or ascendant at 41° north is Scorpio 16°29′ and this increases by 26′ to Scorpio 16°55′ at 40° north. A quarter of the 26′ of increment here or approximately 6′ must therefore be added to Scorpio 16°29′ in order to locate the example ascendant in its zodiacal equivalence at Scorpio 16°35′.

What the beginner must note very carefully at this point is whether he is dealing with mathematical measure on the increase or decrease. What the case may be is always obvious, but it may not be in accordance with expectation to find the zodiacal factor increasing north to south while geographic latitude is decreasing. The phenomenon occurs under certain conditions in polar balance with an opposite occurrence under the complementary situation. Thus he can turn to an Aquarius 27° midheaven in the Tables of Houses where he will see the ascendant increasing south to north with the latitude or from Gemini 21°2' at the 40th parallel to Gemini 21°49' at the 41st.

The minor cusps should present no problem, such as would require particular attention. With a Leo 27° midheaven there is no difference of more than a half degree between the relative positions of any of them at the two adjacent parallels, and the rounding to the next full dgree is quite simple by no more than eye inspection. In using the Dalton tabulations it is necessary to be careful in noting the difference between a decimal point of degree and a presentation of degrees and minutes in columns parallel to each other. Since .1° is 6', the eleventh cusp location at Virgo 29.2° could be expressed at Virgo 29°12'. In this example the rounded zodiacal equivalence of the cusp could be Libra 0° as well as Virgo 30°, but the latter usage is more precise since a zero point of Libra excludes everything possibly comprised in the sign even though Libra 0°0'1" embraces Libra content.

Example II is again a case where only a single adjustment is really necessary in locating the ascendant in its zodiacal correspondence, but in this instance it is the other of the usual two that must be made. The 8' of divergence from 42° north geographic latitude here is less than an eighth of the 60' from 41° north and only needs to be taken into account in much more precise calculation than is worth while in normal course. With an extent of exactitude adequate for the beginner and in instances where the time for calculation is limited, the zodiacal equivalents are taken from the Tables of Houses at 42° north. Quite another matter is the difference between the S.T. of the individual wheel of 4h 26m 55s and the S.T. corresponding to an even Gemini

9° midheaven or 4h 29m 11s. The preceding column for Gemini 8° in the Dalton tabulations shows the equivalent S.T. as 4h 24m 55s. This can be subtracted from the individual S.T. thus:

$$
\begin{array}{ccc}
\text{4h} & \text{26m} & \text{55s} \\
\text{4} & \text{24} & \text{55} \\
\hline
 & 2 &
\end{array}
$$

The S.T. for even Gemini 8° can be subtracted from the S.T. for even Gemini 9° thus:

4h   29m   11s   expressed as

$$
\begin{array}{ccc}
\text{4h} & \text{28m} & \text{71s} \\
\text{4} & \text{24} & \text{55} \\
\hline
 & 4 & 16
\end{array}
$$

In order to arrive at the midheaven of the example horoscope the S.T. must move 2m out of 4m 16s, and for all general purposes this can be taken as a half and a midheaven accepted as Gemini 8°30′ rounded to Gemini 9° as already established.

For the ascendant it can be noted that at 42° north geographic latitude Virgo 11°24′ is the first-house cusp equivalent for a Gemini 8° midheaven, and Virgo 12° 14′ similarly for Gemini 9°. Expressing Virgo 12°14′ as 11°74′ and subtracting 11°24′, the difference of 50′ is the advancement at the ascendant corresponding to 60′ or from Gemini 8° to 9° at the midheaven. The midheaven has been seen to lie approximately halfway in the 60′, and so halfway in the 50′ would be 25′ which added to Virgo 11°24′ becomes the Virgo 11°49′ ascendant accepted for illustrative purposes. The minor cusps are handled in the same fashion. For the eleventh cusp the difference from Cancer 12.6° to Cancer 13.6° is 1.0°, of which half is .5° to be added to Cancer 12.6°. Cancer 13.1° then is rounded, in the special practice presented in these texts, to Cancer 14°.

Example III is close to the situation in the first example, where only the correction for terrestrial latitude was needed for the ascendant and minor houses. But while the S.T. 3h 6m 37s for the individual wheel is almost identical with the 3h 6m 10s of a Taurus 19° midheaven it is slightly more rather than slightly less. Therefore in the recommended practice of the Sabian exposition the cuspal equivalences are rounded to Taurus 20° at the midheaven and nadir and of course if needed for other cusps. Adjustment is much more important for terrestrial latitude in the case of the ascendant and minor cusps because the difference between 55° and 56° north varies from 6' to as much as 36' for these ten of the houses. Birth at 55°45' north is a quarter of a degree in latitude away from the 56th parallel. In Dalton's column for Taurus 19° the first cusp is shown in correspondence with Virgo 1°18' at 56° north and Virgo 0°52' at 55° north. This is a difference of 26', of which a quarter can be taken as 6', and the 6' subtracted from Virgo 1°18' establishes the ascendant at Virgo 1°12'. For determining the minor cusps, at the eleventh it can be seen that the increment between the two geographic parallels is .5° of which a quarter is .1° plus. This subtracted from Gemini 29.9° yields 29.8° and the cusp's zodiacal equivalence is rounded to Gemini 30°.

Example IV duplicates the case of the first and third examples in which only the adjustment for geographic latitude is necessary, and here the adjusting procedure differs in no respect from what has been outlined for the northern hemisphere. In connection with a Sagittarius 13° midheaven taken as a purely mathematical substitute for Gemini 13°, the ascendant at 35° south geographic latitude is shown at Pisces 1°53' representing Virgo 1°53' and at 34° south at Pisces 2°17' representing Virgo 2°17'. The movement between the geographic parallels is thus 24'. Birth at 34°35' south can be taken as halfway between them, and half of 24' or 12' added to Virgo 1°53' locates the ascendant at Virgo 2°5'. The minor cusps are obtained in the same manner illustrated for the eleventh house in connection with the other examples.

It might be well for the beginner to have a clear idea of the extent of apparent zodiacal distortion of house cusps as well illustrated in this instance.

	Northern Hemisphere		*Southern Hemisphere*	
S.T. of midheaven	4h 46m 16s		4h 46m 16s	
Midheaven	Gemini	13°	Gemini	13°
Eleventh house	Cancer	16	Cancer	6
Twelfth house	Leo	17	Cancer	30
Ascendant	Virgo	14 33'	Virgo	2 5'
Second house	Libra	11	Libra	16
Third house	Scorpio	11	Scorpio	19

For the sake of possible greater comprehension of their nature, the two ways in which in their zodiacal correspondence the house cusps other than the tenth and fourth must be corrected at times have been illustrated separately. Where both types of adjustment seem advisable, the operations are merely performed individually and their results added together. Thus, if in the second example it is desired to correct for geographic latitude, the 8' of decrease from the 42d parallel is approximately an eighth of the total difference between the 41st and 42d parallels. As the ascendant for a Gemini 8° midheaven changes position in Virgo between the two parallels by 11', an eighth of that or approximately 1' is subtracted from the ascendant already located by the other correction and the ascendant could be taken somewhat more precisely as Virgo 11°48' rather than Virgo 11°49'.

Calculation from the Rice Tables

The Tables of Houses calculated by Hugh S. Rice present a great difficulty for the beginner since the midheavens and related cusps are presented for each even four minutes of sidereal time rather than for each even midheaven degree of the zodiac. In the first example horoscope the S.T. of the midheaven is 9h 56m 37s. This is between the columns of the Rice house-cusp calculations for a sidereal time of 9h 56m 0s and 10h 0m 0s. The midheaven movement of the example horoscope's S.T. from 9h 56m 0s to 9h 56m 37s is thus 37s out of 4m or 240s of distance from column to column, or in approximate calculation is a little less than a sixth of this distance. The midheavens in zodiacal correspondence for the two positions presented for each 4m in S.T. are respectively Leo 26°46′41″ and Leo 27°49′4″. Expressing this as from 26°46′41″ to 27°48′64″ the zodiacal distance traversed in the 4m of sidereal time is 1°2′23″ that can be expressed as 62′23″ or 60′143″ of which a sixth is approximately 10′24″ to add to Leo 26°46′41″ and give Leo 26°56′65″ or 26°57′5″ to round to Leo 27°.

PUTTING IN THE PLANETS

THE SECOND part in making a horoscope is a more puttering job than the first in actual practice, but it is not nearly as difficult to understand because there are far less details to learn at the beginning or thereafter to continue to take into account. It really provides a much greater interest than establishing the position of the houses in the heavens at a moment and place of birth and then identifying their cusps in the necessary correspondence with the zodiac in which the planets are located, since after all it is only as these astrological significators are finally placed one by one in the wheel-diagram that the horoscopic potentials begin to reveal themselves in very fascinating fashion.

Attention now goes wholly to the ephemeris, and all concern at this point is with the simple interrelations in the zodiac of the celestial factors brought to focus and meaning in a horoscope. The zodiacal positions of the ten major planets commonly employed for astrological analysis are given daily either for the zero hour beginning the day or for noon in the considerable number of ephemerides available as this revision of text is prepared. In all these tabulations in current use the planetary places are shown for the prime meridian established at Greenwich in England, as presumably of the greatest worldwide convenience, and an initial step in locating the significators in the horoscopic wheel-diagram is to make an adjustment to this 0° of geographic longitude thus taken as a basis for the tables.

Although the moon is a satellite of the earth rather than the sun, and the sun in astrology is surrogate for the terrestrial globe through taking on its motion geocentrically, these two bodies while known especially as the lights are not distinguished functionally from the eight true planets given horoscopic consideration. All ten celestial factors are treated alike in the ephemeris.

The Two Phases

There are two quite separate phases in the task of locating the planets in the horoscope. The first is a general adjustment concerning all of them, and the second is the specific calculation for each of them individually. The initial or preliminary attention is demanded by the fact that their positions in the ephemeris are given for a midnight or noon at the Greenwich meridian, and that in the case of virtually any horoscope this is a time quite different from the hour and minute of birth shown locally for the event. Thus when it is one o'clock in the morning in New York City it is around sunrise in London, and this obviously is a very important matter to take into account when using an ephemeris computed for Greenwich. Naturally it would be much too expensive to have a separate set of tables each year for every time zone around the globe. As it happens, the solution of this rather superficial problem is absurdly simple.

The Birth in Greenwich Mean Time

When it comes to finding the places of the planets in the zodiac at the moment of birth, and these are available for midnight or noon at the Greenwich prime meridian in an annual ephemeris, all that is necessary in order to use the tabulations handily is to change the time of birth into the equivalent hours and minutes at Greenwich. The result of this operation is the Greenwich mean time of the given horoscope and this usually is abbreviated as the G.M.T. and in the best practice is noted in or near the basic diagram for purposes of reference along with the S.T. and T.D. and of course the birth data. The T.D. or general time difference between the L.M.T. and the mean time at the Greenwich meridian has already had necessary consideration in putting up the horoscope, since a correction from mean to sidereal measure was necessary in the adjustment for the distance in terrestrial longitude from the prime meridian, and it must now be employed again if for a different purpose.

In the first example horoscope as a case where birth is west of Greenwich or where the sun arrives at the prime meridian first, the T.D. of 4h 56m is added to the L.M.T. of 3:06 p.m. to identify the corresponding Greenwich mean time as 8:02 p.m. Further consideration, in the task of putting in the planets and completing the erection of any horoscope, is with this Greenwich mean time for the individual wheel-diagram at all points. Parenthetically, there is a possibility of confusion on the beginner's part that might lead to a serious misplacement of the fast-moving moon. Ideally the G.M.T. is on the same day as birth, and perhaps in the same division of the day as p.m. for both L.M.T. and G.M.T. in the first example chart. In the fourth example the L.M.T. is a.m. and the G.M.T. is p.m., but on the same day. In the second example the L.M.T. is p.m. and the G.M.T. is a.m. the next day. Difficulty is avoided here if attention is held strictly to the G.M.T. when computing planetary positions. It makes no difference whatsoever if either the G.M.T. or its previous midnight or noon fails to fall in the birthday. The third example as a case of birth east of Greenwich has the possible p.m. birth and a.m. G.M.T. on the same day.

Calculating Planetary Position

The second of the two phases in the task of locating the planets in the horoscope is a separate proposition for each of them because they seldom move through the zodiac at the same rate of speed and in that case cover equal distances in the celestial or zodiacal longitude. The sun has the most regular movement of the ten significators in general acceptance, and can serve well as a preliminary and suppositional example. Thus in 1969 on March 6th at noon Greenwich it is found in Pisces 15°44′33″ and on March 7th at noon Greenwich in Pisces 16°44′34″ or a single second of arc over an even degree of motion. Since 1″ as around a four-thousandth part of its daily movement is altogether too inconsequential to take into account, even if great precision is desired, the daily motion on this date can be taken as an even 1° and for convenience converted to 60′. If it be assumed that somebody is born somewhere on the Greenwich meridian at midnight between March 6th and 7th, the problem of finding the sun's place in his horoscope is simple. Twelve hours have elapsed since the sun was at Pisces 15°44′33″ and it will be twelve hours before it gets to Pisces 16°44′34″. In other words, at the time of birth it has gotten halfway to where it is going in this particular twenty-four hours. In the whole twenty-four it will move the rounded 60′ and in half that time it will move the approximate 30′ or to its horoscopic position of Pisces 16°14′33″ or Pisces 16°15′. The rounding from seconds to minutes is by the usual mathematical procedure explained in connection with putting up the wheel.

The Example Horoscopes

Example I presents a G.M.T. of 8:02 p.m., as already noted in a preceding paragraph. This provides a relatively simple task of calculation of planetary position since in a noon ephemeris a virtually even third of the twenty-four hours has elapsed from the previous noon to the moment of birth. The 2m over the 8h or exact third of a day are only 1/240 of the 8h and consequently of no possible significance. On July 4th at Greenwich noon the sun is at Cancer 12°19′3″ and on the 5th at Greenwich noon it reaches Cancer 13°16′14″. The latter rounds to 13°16′ and then, to permit subtraction, can be taken as 12°76′. The position on the 4th is rounded to 12°19′, which is subtracted from 12°76′ to find the sun's movement in this twenty-four hours to be 57′, and a third of which or 19′ is then found to be the movement from noon to birth and added to Cancer 12°19′ to identify the sun's place in the horoscope as Cancer 12°38′.

One of the most common mistakes made by astrologers, and on rare occasions by the most skillful, is omitting twelve hours in computing the S.T. of the individual midheaven when working from a previous noon found on a prior day for an a.m. L.M.T. As soon as the sun's position has been found in setting up any chart, there should be the quick and easy routine check to make sure the house circle has been placed correctly in the heavens. Obviously the greater light can never be in the fifth house for a midmorning birth. In the present instance the eighth house is a proper place at a midafternoon birth on a day when sunset is at 7:36 p.m. L.M.T.

In the case of this first example, Mercury in twenty-four hours moves from 23°42′ to 25°21′ in Gemini. The July 5th noon position of 25°21′ can be expressed as

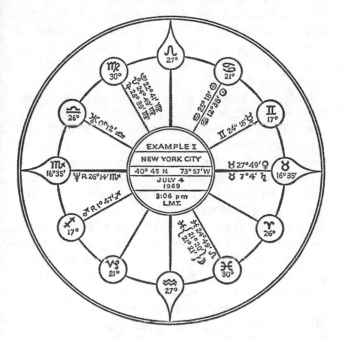

Sidereal time: 9h 56m 37s
Time difference: 4h 56m
Greenwich mean time: 8:02 p.m.

24°81′ from which 23°42′ is subtracted to show 1°39′ or 99′ to be its daily motion. A third of 99′ or 33′ added to Gemini 23°42′ locates the planet in the horoscope at Gemini 23°75′ or 24°15′. Venus similarly is found to have a daily motion of 1°3′ or 63′ of which a third or 21′ is added to Taurus 27°28′ to give its location at Taurus 27°49′.

Mars here becomes an exceptional but not uncommon proposition since the planet is retrograde. The phenomenon of retrogradation has been explained, beginning on page 93, and the calculation of its position involves no difficulty since it is simply performed in reverse. From Sagittarius 1°48′ on July 4th it moves back to Sagittarius 1°45′ by the next noon. This is a movement of 3′ of which a third is 1′. The position in the horoscope therefore is Sagittarius 1°47′ and this is marked with an R to indicate the retrogradation. Something that may be largely a matter of taste, but that at best can be a real refinement of analysis, is attention to the nearness of the stationary point in an immediate past or future. Some astrologers note this by indicating SR for stationary going retrograde or about to go retrograde or recently gone retrograde, and by SD for the contrary case of change to direct motion. This is a subtle point about which the beginner should be informed, but a practice that he might at the start find more confusing than helpful. Mars in this example instance will go direct in four days, but on July 4th it nonetheless is retrograde.

Jupiter moves 7′ in the twenty-four hours and 2′ taken as nearest to an even third establishes its position at Virgo 28°39′. Saturn's daily motion at this time is 5′ of which the nearest third again is 2′ to locate it at Taurus 7°4′. Uranus moves only 1′ forward and Neptune 1′ backward in the twenty-four hours and their positions are taken for the nearest noon or Libra 0°12′

and Scorpio R 26°14′ respectively. Pluto similarly is
Virgo 22°41′. Many old-time astrologers did not trouble themselves to correct the positions of the outermost
planets, but used the nearest position shown in the
ephemeris for their horoscopes. This practice might
never mean any significant neglect of indication, but it
can take the edge off a proper refinement of consideration in respect to aspects and progression.

It may be somewhat more complex to put the moon
in position by this fractional estimation method, but it
does not have to be any more difficult. The moon at
noon on July 5th in this example case lies at Aries
0°24′, and for purposes of subtraction this can be expressed as Pisces 30°24′ and then Pisces 29°84′. Its
position at noon on the 4th at Pisces 16°48′ can thus
be subtracted to reveal a daily motion of 13°36′. Most
simply a third first of the 12° is 4° and of the residue of
1°36′ expressed as 96′ is 32′ as the balance of the third
part sought or a total of 4°32′ to add to Pisces 16°48′
and locate the moon in the wheel-diagram at Pisces
20°80′ or 21°20′.

It is suggested on page 114 that the beginner should
be familiar with three commonly employed zodiacal
factors of relatively minor importance that otherwise
have no consideration in this introductory text. By the
same token however he should know how to locate
them in the horoscopic chart. The moon's node (by
which is meant its north node) is known familiarly as
the dragon's head and is included in the ephemeris, but
its positions are not given for every day. Nonetheless it
is easy to place it in the wheel-diagram by fractional
estimation. Its position at noon on July 3, 1969, is at
Pisces 24°54′ and on July 5th at Pisces 24°47′ by what
is always retrograde motion and therefore not so
marked. This is 7′ of motion for two days, but actually
the movement is only a shade over 3′ a day. The first

example horoscope requires an adjustment of a third of the daily motions of the planets from their place of July 4th, and this place of the north node nearer the noon of the 5th than of the 3d suggests taking two thirds from the position on the 5th. Here 2′ by addition because of the retrograde motion places it at Pisces 24°49′.

The Part of Fortune lies at the distance it must move forward in the zodiac to reach the ascendant that the moon must move similarly to reach its next conjunction with the sun. This is easily calculated by adding the zodiacal longitude in the horoscope of the moon to that of the ascendant, and from the sum subtracting that of the sun to get the zodiacal longitude of the part. Technically this means taking signs and fractions of signs as in usual mathematical procedure, but astrologers find it easier to take the number of the sign in its order in the zodiac and then its degrees and minutes and this produces the same result thus:

Moon		11s	21°	21′	12	21°	21′
Ascendant		7	16	35	8	16	35
		18	37	56	20	37	56
Sun	(−)	3	12	38	(−) 4	12	38
		15	25	18	16	25	18
	or	3	25	18	4	25	18	or Cancer 25°18′

Example II: The T.D. of 5h 51m added to the L.M.T. of 10:09 p.m. gives a G.M.T. of 4:00 a.m. on the next day or December 26th. The elapsed time from the previous noon is thus an even two-thirds of the twenty-four hours. The computations of the first example could be repeated quite precisely by subtracting a third of the daily motions of the planets from their positions at noon on the 26th. Calculating from a midnight ephemeris however can again be by an easy fraction since four hours is a sixth of the twenty-four. The

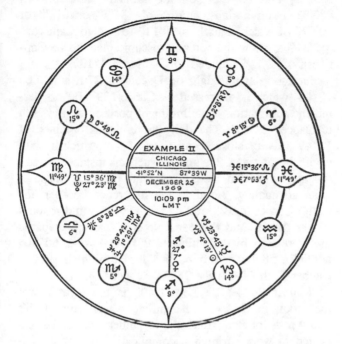

Sidereal time: 4h 26m 55s
Time difference: 5h 51m
Greenwich mean time: 4:00 a.m.

sun at midnight beginning the 27th is at Capricorn 5°3'38" and on the 26th at midnight at Capricorn 4°2'31" with a daily motion of 1°1'7" or 61'7" or 60'67" of which a sixth is 10'11" to add to Capricorn 4°2'31" to show the sun's horoscopic place to be Capricorn 4°12'42" rounded to Capricorn 4°13'.

The moon at midnight on December 27th is at Leo 10°40' which is expressed as Cancer 39°100' to permit the subtraction of its midnight position on the 26th of Cancer 28°51'. The daily motion thus obtained of 11°49' is very close to an even 12° of which a sixth would be an even 2°, and in such an instance as this the approximation would serve all practical purposes quite adequately. Actually the difference between the sixth of an even 12° and of the 11°49' would amount to less than 2' and this example chart can be prepared more precisely by deducting the 2' from 2° or 1°60' and adding 1°58' to the moon's position at midnight on December 26th of Cancer 28°51' to get Cancer 29°109' or Cancer 30°49' or Leo 0°49' as the location for the moon in the second example wheel. But at this point it is obvious that the beginner cannot be expected to work through a complication of approximations with any confidence or competence. Except in such very simple and obvious instances as have been employed to give him the general idea of what he is doing in his calculations, he needs something more fixed or constant in application for the far more unusual computations he will be encountering rather continually. This need is met by the especially calculated diurnal proportional logarithms.

The Use of Logarithms

The beginner is learning to use an ephemeris and a Table of Houses without any necessity of mastering the mathematics behind them, and in the same fashion he can use the special type of logarithms prepared for astrological operations without need to concern himself over the mechanics of applying geometrical proportion to irregularities. He has been dealing on the one side with the daily or twenty-four-hour motion of the planetary bodies, and on the other with the extent to which each planet must move to reach its horoscopic position. He has seen that the factor determining the latter is the time elapsing from the midnight or noon of the ephemeris to the moment of birth, and by the simple device of adding the special logarithm of this lesser time span to the special logarithm of the zodiacal movement of a particular planet in a whole twenty-four hours he has the logarithm of the zodiacal span the planet in question must traverse to reach its horoscopic place.

Thus in connection with the second example chart he can perform the logarithmic calculation as follows:

Moon's daily motion, December 26th:	11° 49′	Logarithm:	.3077
Time elapsed from midnight (26th):	4h	ditto	.7781
By addition:		ditto	1.0858

which shows (nearest to 1.0865) 1°58′ to be the desired movement for the planet in reaching its horoscopic place. This added to the midnight position, Cancer 28°51′, gives Cancer 29°109′ or 30°49′ or Leo 0°49′ in exact agreement with the results of fractional approximation. The logarithmic procedure may take a little more time, but in anything other than the very obvious case of actual simple fractions it is far safer for the beginner.

Returning to *Example I,* the computations for Mercury can be repeated with the use of logarithms, thus:

Mercury's daily motion, July 4th:	1° 39′	Logarithm:	1.1627
Time elapsed from noon (4th):	8h 2m	ditto	.4753
By addition:			1.6380

which shows (nearest to 1.6398) 33′ as the distance the planet must move to its place. This added to the noon position, Gemini 23°42′, gives Gemini 23°75′ or 24°15′ as the horoscopic location of this significator.

Venus can be taken as a further example of calculation for the planets of lesser daily motion, thus:

Daily motion of Venus, July 4th:	1° 3′	Logarithm:	1.3590
Time elapsed from noon (4th):	8h 2m	ditto	.4753
By addition:			1.8343

which shows (nearest to 1.8361) 21′ to be added to the noon position of this planet, Taurus 27°28′, to show its horoscopic place as Taurus 27°49′.

Where the use of logarithms is most helpful in making a horoscope is of course in the calculation of the moon's position, and the procedure is as simple as can be seen again with *Example I* as follows:

Moon's daily motion, July 4th:	13° 36′	Logarithm:	.2467
Time elapsed from noon (4th):	8h 2m	ditto	.4753
By addition:			.7220

which shows (nearest to .7222) 4°33′ to be added to Pisces 16°48′ to locate the planet in the wheel at Pisces 20°81′ or 21°21′ and with a deviation of only 1′ from the result obtained by fractional estimation.

While professionals generally use the logarithms for calculating the moon's position, if at all, beginners tend to employ them for most of the planets. To be noted is that one same logarithm is used for all the significators,

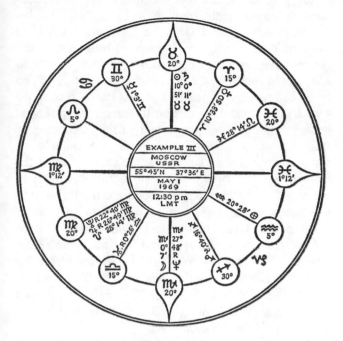

Sidereal time: 3h 6m 37s
Time difference: 2h 30m (minus)
Greenwich mean time: 10:00 a.m.

as .4753 above for the elapsed time from a previous midnight or noon, and in consequence it is often identified as the constant logarithm.

Example III: The T.D. of 2h 30m subtracted from the L.M.T. of 12:30 p.m. because of birth east of the Greenwich prime meridian gives a G.M.T. of 10:00 a.m. on the same day. In this instance the period of two hours before noon means that planets have yet to move a twelfth of their daily motion to reach their places at noon in the noon ephemeris, and so the calculation of their horoscopic positions is most conveniently or commonsensically a matter of subtraction whether the amount of their twenty-four-hour motion not used in gaining their natal places is found by fractional estimation or through the use of logarithms. Mercury's daily motion if using a noon ephemeris is 1°21' or 84' of which a twelfth is 7' and that subtracted from Gemini 1°10' gives Gemini 1°3'. The logarithm for 1°21' or 1.2499 added to the logarithm for 2h or 1.0792 is logarithm 2.3291 for 7'. The beginner must observe that the logarithms still have to be added even if the result is to be subtracted.

Example IV: The T.D. of 3h 53m added to the L.M.T. of 9:37 a.m. gives a G.M.T. of 1:30 p.m. of the same day. With a noon ephemeris the fractional estimation would be on the basis of a sixteenth of the daily motion of each of the planets. It is easier, however, to use more than a single fraction in order to work with readily familiar ones as perhaps taking a twelfth and decreasing it by a quarter of itself or taking a quarter of a quarter. From midnight a half increased by an eighth would be accurate. With slow-moving planets the approximating fractions can become very simple, and for the moon there are always the logarithms.

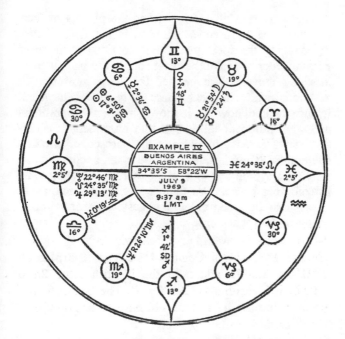

Sidereal time: 4h 46m 14s
Time difference: 3h 53m
Greenwich mean time: 1:30 p.m.

Summary

There are two phases in putting the planets in their places in the horoscope. The first is merely a matter of changing the local mean time to Greenwich mean time in order to make the most simple use of ephemerides now universally computed for the prime meridian at Greenwich. The next phase is taking each planet in turn to find how far it moves in twenty-four hours and what proportional part of that movement is necessary for it to reach its place in the horoscope. The calculations in many instances can be by an uncomplicated fractional estimation, but when there are troublesome irregularities or complex figures as with the moon that always may be a convenient and easy use of the diurnal proportional logarithms.

GLOSSARY

NOTE.—The pronunciations, given only for terms which are alien to everyday non-astrological usage, are from *Webster's International Dictionary of the English Language,* Second Edition, Springfield, Mass., Merriam, 1935, of which Dr. Walter Clyde Curry of Vanderbilt University is Astrological Editor. The respellings are a simplification to avoid the use of diacritical marks. The syllable on which the accent falls is indicated by capital letters.

The Basic Terms

Astrology: the science and art of charting events in human experience, or of analyzing human character, by the cycles of motion and the zodiacal positions of the heavenly bodies.

Natural astrology: astronomy in the simplest sense.

Natal, judicial or genethliac (jeh-NETH-lee-ak) astrology: the fundamental science and art, i.e., the interpretation of a horoscope made for the precise place and time of a person's birth.

Horary (HOE-rah-ree) or divinatory astrology: the interpretation of a special horoscope made for an event, for a query, or for determining a favorable time to act.

Mundane astrology: the interpretation of general human affairs by the horoscopes of political leaders, of historical events and of celestial phenomena, as well as by the altering phases and patterns of celestial phenomena.

Directions, progressions, revolutions and transits: the interpretation of the continuing motion of the heavenly bodies in relation to an original horoscope, or to some prior situation among them.

Horoscope, chart, nativity, figure, map or wheel: the conventionalized diagram of the situation among the moving bodies in the heavens at the moment, and in relation to the place, of an event on the earth; also, sometimes, in the case of the first three terms, the written interpretation of the diagram.

Native: the person for whom a horoscope is made, calculated, cast, erected or put up, and then delineated, read or interpreted.

Astrologer, astrologian (ass-trow-LOW-gee-ann) or (not in good usage) astrologist: the interpreter or practitioner.

The Twelve Signs of the Zodiac

Aries (AYE-ree-eeze, AIR-ee-eeze)
Taurus (TAW-rus)
Gemini (GEM-ee-nigh)
Cancer
Leo
Virgo
Libra (LIE-bra)
Scorpio
Sagittarius (saj-ee-TAY-ree-us)
Capricorn
Aquarius (ah-KWAIR-ee-us)
Pisces (PISS-eeze)

The Ten Planets

The sun	Jupiter
The moon	Saturn
Mercury	Uranus (YOU-rah-nus)
Venus	Neptune
Mars	Pluto

One Hundred and Fifty Technical Terms, Commonly Encountered

Above the earth: the area in the houses counterclockwise from the descendant to the ascendant; the southern hemisphere.

Accidental dignity: the favorable position of a planet by house or aspect.

Affliction: an unfavorable aspect or situation in the horoscope.

Air: the triplicity of the signs associated with autumn.

Almuten (al-MEW-ten): the strongest planet in the chart in terms of accidental and essential dignities.

Anareta (ah-NAR-ee-ta): the planet concerned in death; see also "hyleg."

Angle, angular: a house, or house relationship, at the horizon and meridian, an indication of a focalized emphasis in human affairs.

Application: a planet's movement towards a given aspect.

Ascendant, ascendent: the horizon at the east in the horoscope, the cusp of the first house, and the first house itself.

Aspect: a geometrical relationship between planets in the ecliptic, such as the "major aspects" of conjunction, sextile, square, trine and opposition; also known as "configuration" and "familiarity."

Aspectarian (ass-peck-TARE-ee-ann): a tabulation of culminating aspects by day and hour for convenience in reference.

Below the earth: the area in the houses counterclockwise from the ascendant to the descendant; the northern hemisphere.

Cadent (KAY-dent): a house relationship of direct subordination to the angles, an indication of dependence in human affairs.

Cardinal: the quadrature of the signs associated with the equinoxial and solstitial points in the heavens, an indication of the factor of change in experience; also known as "moveable."

Cazimi (KAZ-i-mee): see "combust."

Celestial equator: the path of the earth's rotation on its axis, the "circle of the houses."

Chaldean order: see "planet."

Circle: the astrological symbol for a "higher" or "spiritual" reference; also often the houses, or signs, or both together.

Combust (kom-BUST): a planet weakened by conjunction with the sun; but strengthened if within 17' of exact, which is then known as "cazimi."

Common: the quadrature of the signs directly subordinate to the cardinal group, or an indication of the factor of adaptability in experience; also known as "mutable."

Configuration: an aspect or aspects; a pattern in the horoscope.

Conjunction: the aspect where the planets are at approximately the same place in the zodiac.

Constellation: a group of stars, usually arranged in an identifiable pattern; specifically, such groups as they originally identified the signs of the zodiac, or the "natural zodiac."

Cosmic cross: a pattern of the planets in which quadrature is emphasized, including both the t-cross and the x-cross.

Crescent: the symbol of the moon; more generally, a representation of soul or personality.

Critical degrees: the places of certain fixed stars regarded as of particular import; also the cusps of the lunar mansions.

Cross: the symbol for matter, or for a "lower" or physical reference; also a shortened term for cosmic cross.

Cusp: the line at which a house begins or is defined.

Debility: the unfavorable position of a planet in a reverse of "dignity," such as "detriment" or "fall."

Decanate (DECK-a-nate): one third of a sign, named from its decan or ruler, known also as decan, decant or face and involved in much difference of opinion; in the most general modern practice, the rulership of the first third of a sign by its own nature and lord, and the next thirds in order by the succeeding signs of the same triplicity in the terms of their natures and lords.

Declination: the angle between the planes of a planet's orbit and the earth's equator, measured in degrees of arc on the hour-circle where the planet is situated.

Degree: one thirtieth of a sign of the zodiac or one three-hundred-and-sixtieth of a circle; in the zodiac, a special narrow unit which has been given significance by the tabulation of particular cases of characteristic emphasis, and by the expression of degree differentiation through a system of symbolical interpretation.

Descendant: the horizon at the west in a horoscope, the cusp of the seventh house, and the seventh house itself.

Determinator: an astrological factor with a particular significance; see "focal determinator."

Detriment: a planet weakened by its place in a sign opposite a sign it "rules."

Dignity: see "accidental dignity," "essential dignity"; also known as "fortitude."

Direct: a planet's forward or normal motion, counterclockwise in the zodiac.

Directions: the projection of the horoscopic relationships into time cycles of the unfolding life and experience according to an equation of four minutes after birth corresponding to a year of life, which creates the relatively little used "primary directions," or an equation of a day after birth corresponding to a year of life, which is the commonly used system of "secondary directions"; together with expansions and modifications of these procedures; also known, in whole or in part, as "progressions."

Disposition: the rule of one planet by another when the former lies in a sign "ruled" by the latter.

Diurnal (die-UR-nal): see "rotation."

Dragon's head: the moon's north node, or the ascending node given in an ephemeris, usually taken as a point of protection in the horoscope.

Dragon's tail: the moon's south node, exactly opposite the north node, usually taken as a point of self-undoing or "spiritual opportunity" in the horoscope.

Earth: the triplicity of the signs associated with winter; also, occasionally, the horizon, as in the phrases "above the earth" and "below the earth."

Eclipse: a lunation of extra significance in astrology, when both sun and moon are in a line of observation from the earth; with effects traditionally said to have duration of a year for every hour the sun is eclipsed, and of a month for every hour the moon is eclipsed.

Ecliptic (ee-CLIP-tick): the orbit of the earth and apparent orbit of the sun; thus the zodiac, or the "circle of the signs," sometimes specifically designated as the "fixed zodiac"; see also "constellation."

Election: a horary chart cast in advance to aid in determining the proper time for a given action; more correctly, "radical election."

Element: usually a "triplicity"; sometimes any distinguishing quality, as of a planet.

Elevated: position in the houses near the midheaven or upper meridian.

Ephemeris; plural, ephemerides (eh-FEM-er-iss; eff-ee-MARE-uh-deez): a tabulation of the planets' places, together with relative data.

Equator: the central line around the earth midway between the poles; also the projection of its plane into the heavens as the path of the earth's rotation on its axis, the "circle of the houses."

Equinox (EE-kwee-nocks; ECK-wee-nocks): a point where the ecliptic and equator cross in the heavens; sometimes specifically the vernal equinox, or Aries 0°, but equally properly the autumnal equinox, or Libra 0°.

Essential dignity: the favorable position of a planet by sign, as place in a sign it "rules" or in a sign in which it is "exalted."

Exaltation: certain special places of strength for the planets, as Aries for the sun, omitted from this book as of no great value to beginners.

Fall: a planet weakened by its place in a sign opposite its "exaltation."

Familiarity: an old term for "aspect."

Fanhandle: a special pattern of the planets in which a "singleton" is given added significance by the regularity of arrangement in a group of planets opposite to it.

Feminine signs: the water-earth group, or Taurus, Cancer, Virgo, Scorpio, Capricorn and Pisces.

Fire: the triplicity of the signs associated with spring.

Fixed: the quadrature of the signs which provides the projection of the cardinal group, an indication of the defining factor in experience.

Fixed stars: the brighter or more prominent stars, other than planets, which by zodiacal place, or projection on the ecliptic in longitude, are given

particular astrological indication or importance,
such as the Pleiades in Taurus 27°.

Fixed zodiac: see "ecliptic."

Focal determinator: an underlying or basic pattern in
the horoscope, the indicator of an effective focus
in a native's life as a guide to perspective in astrological delineation.

Fortitude: see "dignity."

Geocentric: the normal astrological point of view,
with the earth as the center of human experience
taken as the basis for astronomical observation.

Grand trine: a chain of trines around the wheel.

Head: see "dragon's head."

Heliocentric: an astrological point of view sometimes
advocated, with a hypothetical center of experience and measurement taken in the sun.

Hemisphere emphasis: all planets east, west, south or
north; or similarly placed in any definable half of
the wheel.

Horizon: the ascendant and descendant; in astrology,
the plane of observation and the ground of experience.

Hour: see "planetary hour."

House: one of the twelve divisions of the celestial
equator, similar to the division of the ecliptic or
zodiac into signs, and numbered one to twelve
counterclockwise from the ascendant; also a sign
of the zodiac of which a given planet is ruler.

Hyleg, hylegiacal (HIGH-leg; high-lee-JYE-a-cal):
the planet principally concerned with giving life,
or the places in the horoscope which convey the

life-giving power, omitted from this book as of little value to a beginner; also known as "apheta" or "prorogator."

Interception: the situation of a sign wholly between the cusps of two adjacent houses, so that it does not appear on any cusp; also the situation of any planet placed in such a sign.

Latitude: on the earth's surface, distance in degrees north or south from the equator; in the heavens, the angle between the planes of a planet's orbit and the ecliptic or earth's orbit, measured in degrees of arc on the hour-circle where the planet is situated.

Lights: the sun and moon; also commonly, the "luminaries."

Long ascension: the signs Cancer through Sagittarius, which take longer in rising daily at the eastern horizon, and give a greater fluidity in general experience.

Longitude: on the earth's surface, distance in degrees east and west from the meridian of Greenwich; in the heavens, distance in degrees counterclockwise in the circle of the zodiac from the vernal equinox, or Aries 0°.

Lord: a planet as "ruler" of a sign, house or other planet.

Luminaries: see "lights."

Lunar mansion: see "mansion."

Lunation: the moment of conjunction of the sun and moon, and the time interval between successive conjunctions; also the chart for the moment of a lunation at any given place.

Mansion: a house, or sign of the zodiac; sometimes specifically the sign ruled by a given planet; more particularly, the twenty-eight divisions in the zodiac of the moon's monthly course through the heavens, or the "lunar mansions" which establish "critical degrees" of the zodiac at the point of each of the twenty-eight cusps.

Masculine signs: the fire-air group, or Aries, Gemini, Leo, Libra, Sagittarius and Aquarius.

Meridian: the circle of longitude in the zodiac, and of right ascension or sidereal time in the celestial equator, which passes through the point overhead; also any half-circle by which terrestrial longitude is indicated on the earth's surface.

Midheaven: the upper meridian in the horoscope, the cusp of the tenth house, or the tenth house itself; also known as the *"medium coeli"* or *"M.C."*

Moveable: see "cardinal."

Mutable: see "common."

Mutual reception: two planets, each in a sign ruled by the other, with a consequent strengthening of both.

Nadir (NAY-dur; NAY-deer): the lower meridian in the horoscope, the cusp of the fourth house, or the fourth house itself; also known as the *"imum coeli,"* or *"I.C."*

Natural zodiac: the constellations of stars in the heavens which originally, some two thousand years ago, identified the signs of the zodiac and served as an "ephemeris in the skies."

Node: the point where the orbit of another heavenly body intersects the ecliptic; in astrology, usually

the moon's ascending or north node, the "dragon's head," if not indicated otherwise.

Obliquity of the ecliptic (ob-LICK-wee-tee): the angle between the planes of the earth's orbit and
celestial equator; in 1940 it is 23°, 27', 49.5" and
diminishing .47" a year.

Occidental: the area in the houses counterclockwise
from the nadir to the midheaven; the western
hemisphere.

Opposition: the aspect where the planets are approximately opposite each other in the zodiac.

Orb of influence: the degree of deviation from exactness allowed planets in aspect; usually shortened
to "orb."

Orbit: the path of one heavenly body in revolution
around another; in the case of the earth around
the sun, the ecliptic or zodiac.

Oriental: the area in the houses counterclockwise from
the midheaven to the nadir; the eastern hemisphere.

Parallel of declination: a sixth and final "major aspect," omitted from this book as of no great value
to a beginner, indicated by a "P" and occurring
when two planets have the same declination, irrespective of whether this be north or south; usually known simply as "parallel," and in such a
case not to be confused with other forms of parallel in primary directions.

Part: a symbolical point expressing the relationship
between any two planets or other astrological factors as the distance between them, when this distance is projected counterclockwise in longitude

from the ascendant to establish the point in question.

Part of Fortune, pars fortuna: the one "part" in rather universal use, usually taken as an indication of the fundamental focus of self-interest in the life. The counterclockwise distance from the sun to the moon is projected counterclockwise from the ascendant.

Planet: one of the heavenly bodies with a regular movement across the face of the "fixed stars," in astrology including the sun, whose apparent motion in the zodiac is really that of the earth, and the moon, which is a satellite of the earth rather than the sun, but excluding the asteroids and periodic comets; the seven bodies of the original system which, in the "Chaldean order" that links the planetary days and hours, are Saturn, Jupiter, Mars, sun, Venus, Mercury and moon, and by "extended Chaldean order" include Pluto, Neptune, Uranus and the original seven in the same sequence.

Planetary days: the rule of each day by the planet which has named it, as Sunday by the sun, Monday by the moon, Tuesday by Mars (from Tiu, the war-god also known as Tiwaz and Tyr), Wednesday by Mercury (from Woden, i.e., Odin), Thursday by Jupiter (from Thor), Friday by Venus (from Freya, or Frigga), and Saturday by Saturn.

Planetary hours: the division of the daily periods between sunrise and sunset, and between sunset and sunrise, into twelve "hours" each, under the rulership of the planets in original Chaldean order beginning at sunrise with the planet ruling the day and continuing on in an infinite sequence.

Prenatal epoch: see "rectification."

Primary directions: see "directions."

Progressed horoscope: a wheel calculated for a given period of life in secondary directions.

Progressions: practically a synonymous term for "directions," but with specific reference among some astrological groups.

Quadrature: the classification of the signs in groups of four on the basis of their conformity to the axes of the equinoxial and solstitial points in the ecliptic, or their deviation from them; specifically the distinction among the signs as "cardinal," "fixed" and "common"; also sometimes the square aspect.

Quartile (KWOR-tul): see "square."

Querent (KWEER-ent): the person who asks a horary question.

Quincunx (KWIN-kungks): a minor aspect in which planets are approximately five signs apart, or 150°, or a semisextile beyond the trine and in nature and strength similar to the semisextile.

Quintile (KWIN-tul): a minor aspect when planets are approximately one fifth of a circle apart, or 72°; also creating the "semiquintile" or "decile" of 36° separation, and the "biquintile" of 144° separation; indications of various phases of personal talent.

Radical: in horary astrology, the competency of a chart for judgment.

Rectification: the art of correcting a horoscope of uncertain time, or of rectifying errors in its calculation, through a comparison of its testimony with the events of the native's life, or by some equivalent technique such as the determination of the "prenatal epoch."

Retrograde: a planet moving backwards in the zodiac, a phenomenon due to the angle of observation from the earth.

Revolution: the time in which a star or planet revolves around the sun or the earth; a horoscope erected for the return of a body to its place in a natal figure, or rather commonly the "solar revolution" erected annually for the sun's return; also the sun's return to a zodiacal point as the "ingress charts" for the equinoxial and solstitial points, and by extension the ingress of any or all planets into a sign; and very commonly the return of the moon to a conjunction with the sun, or the "lunation chart."

Right ascension: measurement counterclockwise on the celestial equator in degrees from the vernal equinox, equivalent to sidereal time.

Rising: position in the houses near the ascendant, usually referring to one particular planet below the horizon and closer to the ascendant than any others.

Rotation: the time in which a heavenly body makes a complete turn on its own axis, the diurnal as compared with the annual motion of the earth.

Ruler: a planet specially assigned to one or two of the signs, as Mars to Aries, and by extension ruler also of the house or houses on whose cusp or cusps the sign or signs will appear, and of any other planets contained within a sign so ruled; also known as "lord."

Secondary directions: see "directions."

Semisextile: a minor aspect in which planets are at approximately the same point in adjacent signs, a half-sextile and of similar nature to the sextile but weaker.

Semisquare: a minor aspect in which the planets are approximately a sign and a half apart, a half-square and of similar nature to the square but weaker; also known as an "octile."

Separation: a planet's movement away from a given aspect.

Septile (SEP-tul): a minor aspect when planets are approximately one seventh of a circle apart, or about 51°, an indication of fatality.

Sesquiquadrate, sesquiquartile: a minor aspect in which the planets are at the approximate distance of a square and a semisquare, or 135°, in strength and nature similar to the semisquare.

Sextile (SEKS-tul): an aspect in which the planets are related by sympathetic triplicity or half trine, or are approximately separated by the sixth part of the zodiac.

Short ascension: the signs Capricorn through Gemini, which take less time in rising daily at the eastern horizon, and give a greater self-containment in general experience.

Sidereal time (sigh-DEAR-ee-al): in astrology, a way of indicating distance around the circle of the houses or celestial equator, counterclockwise from the vernal equinox, by hours and minutes instead of degrees, exactly equivalent to right ascension

Sign of the zodiac: one of the twelvefold divisions of the zodiacal circle; usually just "sign."

Significator: a planet with certain specific importance, sometimes a house or sign in the same sense; also known as a "promittor."

Singleton: a single planet in a hemisphere of the horoscope.

Solstice (SOL-stiss): a point in the ecliptic farthest from the celestial equator, specifically the summer solstice at Cancer 0° and the winter solstice at Capricorn 0°.

Speculum: a tabulation of various important elements in a horoscope, especially used in connection with primary directions.

Square: an aspect where the planets are approximately at right angles to each other, or at quarter points on the circle, and so related by cross-stress in a similarity of quadrature; also known as "quartile," "quadrate" and "quadrature."

Stationary: a planet without zodiacal motion at a given moment, a phenomenon due to the angle of observation from the earth.

Stellium: a cluster of planets in any one sign or house.

Succedent (suck-SEE-dent): a house relation which provides a projection of the angles, an indication of potentiality in affairs.

Symbolical degrees: see "degree."

Tables of Houses: a calculation of the correspondence of the house cusps to the signs according to the modification of the horizon, and houses other than the tenth and fourth, by the geographic latitude.

Tail: see "dragon's tail."

Transits: interpretation of a horoscope by the correspondences between its factors and the place of the planets in the heavens at the actual time of investigation, together with judgments based on the current relations among the planets themselves.

Translation of light: a planet moving from its aspect to another planet into its aspect to a third, when neither of the two other planets are in proper orb of aspect, thereby bringing about the effect of an actual aspect between them.

Trine: an aspect in which planets are related by triplicity, or are separated by approximately a third part of the zodiac.

Triplicity (tri-PLISS-i-tee): the classification of the signs in groups of three on the basis of their affinity to the four seasonal points in the ecliptic; specifically the distinction among the signs as "fire," "water," "air" and "earth."

Via combusta: from Libra 15° through Scorpio 15°, used in horary astrology.

Void of course: when a planet makes no aspect before it leaves the sign in which it is found, a detail of importance in horary astrology.

Water: the triplicity of the signs associated with summer.

Zodiac: see "ecliptic," also "constellation."

INDEX

THE HOROSCOPES

POINTS IN DELINEATION

THE FOCAL DETERMINATORS

THE TABULATIONS

THE BASIC EXPLANATIONS

ADDITIONAL EXAMPLES OF SUN-SIGNS

ADDITIONAL POINTS OF GENERAL REFERENCE

NOTES

NOTES

NOTES

NOTES

NOTES

NOTES